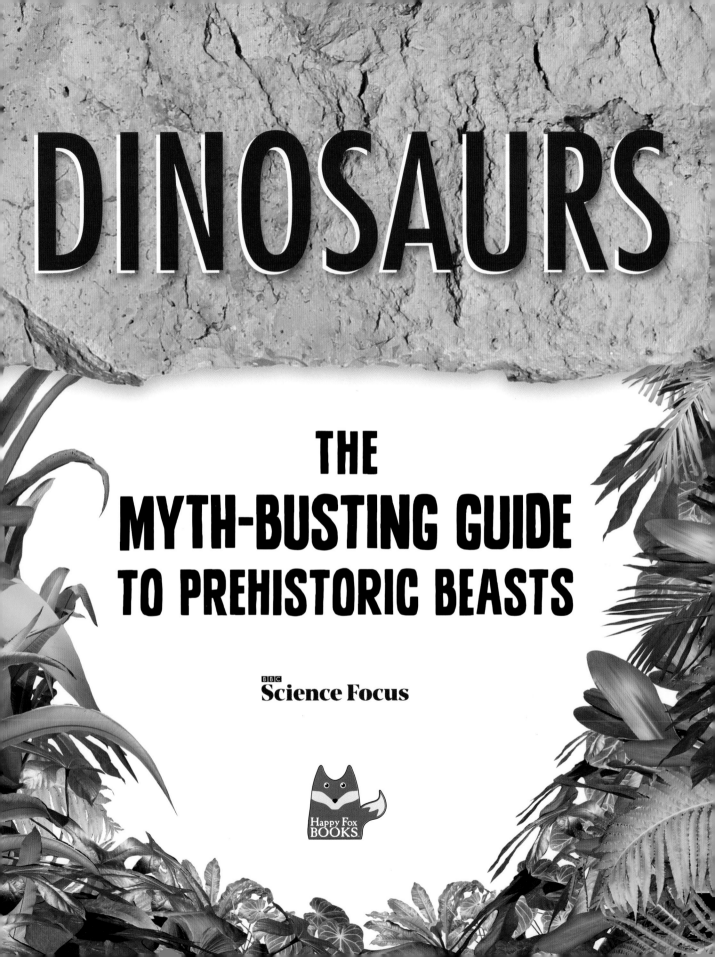

DINOSAURS

THE
MYTH-BUSTING GUIDE
TO PREHISTORIC BEASTS

BBC
Science Focus

Happy Fox
BOOKS

Dinosaurs: The Myth-Busting Guide to Prehistoric Beasts

Happy Fox Books Project Team

Vice President – Content: Christopher Reggio
Editor: Laura Taylor
Copyeditor: Katie Ocasio
Designer: Mary Ann Kahn

BBC Science Focus/Immediate Media Project Team

Editorial
Editor: Daniel Bennett
Managing Editor: Alice Lipscombe-Southwell
Production Editor: Jheni Osman
Commissioning Editor: Jason Goodyer
Editorial Assistant: James Lloyd
Additional Copy: Josie Clarkson

Art & Pictures
Art Editor: Joe Eden
Designers: Steve Boswell, Jenny Price, Dean Purnell
Picture Editor: James Cutmore

First published in 2019 in North America by Happy Fox Books, an imprint of Fox Chapel Publishing Company, Inc., 903 Square Street, Mount Joy, PA 17552.

ISBN 978-1-64124-031-4 (paperback)
ISBN 978-1-64124-045-1 (hardcover)

The Cataloging-in-Publication data is on file with the Library of Congress.

To learn more about the other great books from Fox Chapel Publishing, or to find a retailer near you, call toll-free 800-457-9112 or visit us at *www.FoxChapelPublishing.com*.

We are always looking for talented authors. To submit an idea, please send a brief inquiry to acquisitions@foxchapelpublishing.com.
Fox Chapel Publishing makes every effort to use environmentally friendly paper for printing.

Printed in Singapore

While every attempt has been made to ensure that the content of *Dinosaurs: The Myth-Busting Guide to Prehistoric Beasts* was as accurate as possible at the time of publication, some information contained herein may have since become out of date. Also, the content of certain sections is occasionally subject to interpretation; in these cases, the most respected source was favored.

WELCOME . . .

. . . TO A NEW AGE OF DINOSAURS—the age of discovery. In the last 20 years, about three-quarters of all known dinosaur species have been found, and a new species is discovered almost every week. Indeed, dinosaurs are being unearthed at such an incredible rate that I'm half hoping one day I'll walk out the front door and trip on what looks like a 6½ foot (2m)-long *Brachiosaurus* bone, only to find that I've stumbled on a whole new species. (*Bennettosaurus* does have a nice ring to it.)

The wealth of new specimens is keeping paleontologists busy—plenty of fodder for all sorts of new theories about what dinosaurs looked like and how they lived. This book reports on the latest findings, busting a few dino myths along the way.

Journey back in time to discover the key moments in our planet's history that led to the birth and death of these prehistoric marvels (page 6). Find out how they managed to conquer the world, going from being small, furtive animals to a dominant global force (page 16). Discover the very latest research on what they looked like (page 26). Find out how animals living today are being used to imagine how dinosaurs lived all those millennia ago (page 38). Learn about the day the dinosaurs died (page 64) and what if that ill-fated asteroid hadn't hit the Yucatan peninsula at that precise time, but had strayed into the deep ocean just a few moments later (page 76). And, finally, discover how we could clone a "dinosaur light" version of *Velociraptor* and build a real Jurassic Park (page 88).

Immerse yourself in this ultimate guide to the latest research on dinosaurs and prepare to be amazed by the secret lives of these incredible beasts.

Daniel Bennett, Editor

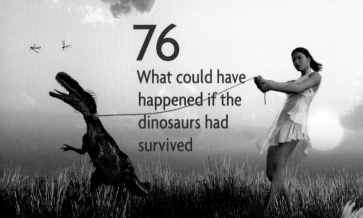

76
What could have happened if the dinosaurs had survived

16
How dinosaurs came to rule the planet

64
How an asteroid strike killed off the dinosaurs

26
The latest research into what dinosaurs looked like

CONTENTS

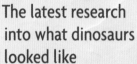

EARTH THROUGH THE AGES

Take a journey through time and the key moments in our planet's history that led to the birth and death of the dinosaurs

MYA = Million Years Ago

PRECAMBRIAN
4,600-542 MYA

4,000-2,500 MYA
Archean

4,600 MYA
FORMATION OF THE SOLAR SYSTEM

After the Big Bang (13.8 billion years ago) when our universe was born, it was many billions of years before our solar system started to develop. Then around 4,600 MYA, a giant molecular cloud, full of hydrogen, began to collapse under the pull of gravity. Most of the molecules fell to the center to create our sun, while the remainder flattened out into a spinning disk, out of which the planets (including Earth), moons, and asteroids in our solar system formed.

4,550 MYA
EARTH'S FORMATION

The solar wind swept away lighter elements like hydrogen, and Earth (along with Mars, Venus, and Mercury) formed as the remaining heavier rocky materials clumped together under gravity. Over time the densest material sank to the center of the Earth, while the lighter pieces rose up from the crust. Around 50 million years later, Earth is thought to have collided and melded together with another planet—Theia. Huge amounts of debris were thrown out from the collision, some of which stuck together to become Earth's moon. The gravitational pull of the moon helped to stabilize Earth's rotation and get the planet's climate under control.

2,500-542 MYA
Proterozoic

542-488 MYA
Cambrian

3,500 MYA
FIRST LIFE

3,500-million-year-old algal mats are the earliest definite evidence of life, though some think it could be as old as 4,400 million years. With no atmospheric oxygen, these organisms probably lived on a chemical soup from underwater vents.

715–600 MYA
SNOWBALL EARTH

Earth was coated in ice—thought to be triggered by rapid weathering of the continents sucking carbon dioxide out of the atmosphere. Temperatures plummeted to -4°F (-20°C) at the equator. Most life was wiped out.

4,400 MYA
FIRST CONTINENTS AND OCEANS

None of Earth's original crust remains today, but we've found a few crystals from the original, deep in hills in Western Australia. The chemistry of these crystals, known as zircons, reveals that by this time Earth had a continental crust and, crucially for life, oceans made of water.

4,000 MYA
PLATE TECTONICS BEGINS

As Earth cooled, we think that the mantle began to move in predictable patterns, driving the jigsaw of sliding plates. This active surface helps to stabilize the planet's temperature and recycles chemical elements, and is believed to be crucial in making it habitable for life.

Stromatolites, created by blue-green algae, in Shark Bay, Western Australia.

2,400 MYA
GREAT OXYGENATION EVENT

Oxygen began to accumulate in the atmosphere when photosynthesizing bacteria started to dominate. Using the sun's energy to convert carbon dioxide and water into food, they produced oxygen as waste.

◀ A fossilized trilobite. Now extinct, trilobites are thought to have lived on the sea floor.

560 MYA
CAMBRIAN EXPLOSION

As Earth exited the Snowball (probably aided by volcanic activity), life leapt forward with multicellular creatures evolving rapidly. By 530 million years ago the first animals were scuttling onto land.

▼ Cross-section of a subduction zone, where one tectonic plate slides under another.

PALEOZOIC
542–251 MYA

488-443 MYA	443-416 MYA	416-359 MYA	359-299 MYA	299-251 MYA
Ordovician	Silurian	Devonian	Carboniferous	Permian

470 MYA
FIRST LAND PLANTS
Moss-like plants crept onto land. These early plants didn't have deep roots, but the acids they secreted dissolved the rocks they were clinging onto. The rock weathering sucked carbon dioxide out of the atmosphere, triggering another ice age and extinction event.

447-443 MYA
ORDOVICIAN-SILURIAN MASS EXTINCTION EVENT
The proto-continent Gondwana moved toward the South Pole. This, along with rock weathering, resulted in global cooling and a drop in sea level. Most life was marine and about 85% of it vanished.

Corals, like *Streptelasma divaricans*, were decimated by this extinction event.

After the supercontinent Pangaea broke apart into Laurasia and Gondwana, the latter headed south.

375-360 MYA
LATE DEVONIAN MASS EXTINCTION EVENT
About 70% of all species died in a series of extinction pulses. Marine life was hit hard, with coral reefs disappearing. Life may have been the cause—the rise of plants with roots disrupting rocks, leading to reduced atmospheric carbon dioxide and cooling.

252 MYA
PERMIAN-TRIASSIC MASS EXTINCTION EVENT
The worst extinction event of all time, killing 90% to 96% of species. The cause is debated, but it could have been a meteorite, volcanic action, or methane release that led to rapid climate change. Life took about 10 million years to recover.

The saber-toothed, mammal-like reptile *Dinogorgon* was one of the casualties of this extinction event.

Life was its own worst enemy— early plants released acids that ultimately caused carbon dioxide depletion.

251-246 MYA	246-229 MYA	229-200 MYA
Early Triassic	Mid Triassic	Late Triassic

Two *Herrerasaurus* pursue a *Silesaurus* in a scene from the Late Triassic.

214 MYA

Plateosaurus lived in herds. Graveyards, where more than 55 individuals are preserved together, show where they became stuck in the mud and starved to death.

201 MYA

TRIASSIC-JURASSIC MASS EXTINCTION EVENT

Between 70% and 75% of Earth's species went extinct at the end of the Triassic, including many amphibians and large reptiles. The cause is unknown, but the empty niches allowed dinosaurs to proliferate in the Jurassic.

245 MYA

DINOSAUR ANCESTORS

Archosaurs ("ruling reptiles") evolved around 245 million years ago. They are the ancestors of dinosaurs and pterosaurs (flying reptiles) as well as modern-day crocodiles and birds.

231–228 MYA

Eoraptor was one of the first dinosaurs. The carnivore or omnivore had both curved and leaf-shaped crowns. Its hands had five digits, but two of these were clawless stumps. Only juveniles have been found so far.

243 MYA

FIRST DINOSAUR

The dog-sized *Nyasasaurus* is either the oldest known dinosaur or the closest known relative to the earliest dinosaurs, preceding any other dinosaur by 12 million years.

Dinosaurs, such as *Dilophosaurus*, prospered after the Triassic-Jurassic Mass Extinction Event.

200-175 MYA
Early Jurassic

175-161 MYA
Mid Jurassic

The shrew-like *Juramaia sinensis* is thought to have been the earliest "true" mammal.

200 MYA
FIRST MAMMALS

Dinosaurs began to dominate on land, but one group of mammal-like reptiles found their own successful niche. The tiny mouse-sized creatures tended to live in trees, feed on plants and insects, and hunted at night when the dinosaurs were less active. These creatures are the ancestors of all mammals.

155–145 MYA

Coelurus was small with hollow bones and long legs, making it dainty and fast. It lived in what is now North America and hunted smaller animals, gripping them with its three long claws.

150–135 MYA

Hylaeosaurus was one of the first three fossils that led Victorian scientist Richard Owen to realize that certain fossil reptiles represented a brand new group—dinosaurs.

Hylaeosaurus (below left) and *Iguanodon* (below right) were herbivores from the Early Cretaceous.

Coelurus was a feisty little carnivore from the Late Jurassic.

156-144 MYA

Stegosaurus was a large dinosaur with a tiny brain the size of a lime. Its plates were most likely used for display, but possibly also for controlling body temperature.

147 MYA

Archaeopteryx was a small, carnivorous bird-like dinosaur, weighing just 18 oz (500g), that lived during the Late Jurassic. It is frequently described as the "missing link" between dinosaurs and birds.

135–125 MYA

Iguanodon was a 5.5-ton (5-tonne) herbivore with a vicious spike for a thumb that almost certainly served as a weapon.

125–122 MYA

Caudipteryx had a fan-like array of large tail feathers, probably used in display like a peacock.

Caudipteryx was probably unable to fly.

95–70 MYA

Spinosaurus had a gigantic sail extending along its back, supported internally by tall, bony spines that grew upward from its backbone.

Spinosaurus was the largest carnivorous dinosaur that ever lived—bigger than T. rex.

101–66 MYA
Late Cretaceous

90 MYA

Argentinosaurus was the heaviest (154,000 lbs/70,000kg) and longest (115 ft/35m) land animal ever discovered, laying eggs the size of footballs.

68–66 MYA

Triceratops, meaning three-horned face, had up to 800 teeth and a large frill to protect its neck and attract mates. Bite marks and broken horns show it sometimes fell prey to *T. rex*.

68–66 MYA

Tyrannosaurus is surely the most infamous dinosaur. With its 60 saw-edged teeth, it could bite through bone.

68–66 MYA

Ankylosaurus was a formidable beast with a hefty clubbed tail and layers of bone within its skin, known as osteoderms.

66–23 MYA Paleogene	66–56 MYA Paleocene	56–34 MYA Eocene	34–23 MYA Oligocene	23–2.5 MYA Neogene	23–5 MYA Milocene	5–2.5 MYA Pliocene	2.5 MYA–Present Quaternary	2.5 MYA–11,700 Pleistocene	11,700–Present Holocene

Volcanic action warmed up the planet, creating ice-free poles.

56 MYA
PALEOCENE-EOCENE THERMAL MAXIMUM

Crocs basked on Alaskan beaches and palm trees flourished in the Arctic. There was no ice at either of the poles. Earth's average temperature was nearly 73°F (23°C) (today's is around 57°F [14°C]). Volcanoes likely triggered this warm episode, which was followed by a cycle of ice ages.

66 MYA
CRETACEOUS-TERTIARY MASS EXTINCTION EVENT

Quite possibly the most famous mass extinction event. An asteroid impact, probably followed by volcanic eruptions, killed off the dinosaurs and about 75% of species. Since then, birds and mammals have evolved to become the dominant land species.

A larger brain helped *Homo sapiens* store more information and solve more complex problems.

200,000 years ago
EVOLUTION OF MAN

Over four million years ago our earliest ape-like ancestors began to walk upright across the African plains. Around 200,000 years ago, our own species, *Homo sapiens*, emerged. Then, 70,000 years ago, we ventured out of Africa and quickly came to dominate every continent in the world, except Antarctica.

TYRANNOSAURUS REX

THE "TYRANT LIZARD" WAS ONE OF THE MOST FEROCIOUS PREDATORS OF ALL TIME—EVERYONE GAVE THIS FEARSOME BEAST A WIDE BERTH.

IN ADULTS, MOST OF THE SKIN WAS PROBABLY SCALY, BUT DOWNY-LIKE FEATHERS POSSIBLY RAN ALONG THE SPINE.

With a bite three times stronger than a lion's, and around 60 saw-edged teeth each measuring up to 8 inches (20cm) long, *T. rex* could chomp through bone. It hunted some of the largest and most heavily armored dinosaurs around. But it also scavenged for food—the part of the brain responsible for smell was fairly large, meaning it could sniff out carcasses.

Groups of skeletons from close relatives of *T. rex* have been found, suggesting *T. rex* might have also hunted in packs. Fossil evidence of bite marks from other tyrannosaurs show they definitely fought one another, competing for food or mates. And there is even some evidence that *T. rex* indulged in a spot of cannibalism.

APPROXIMATE SIZE COMPARISON

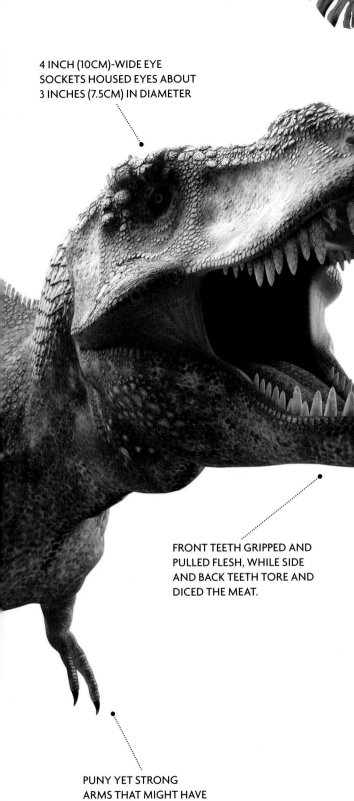

4 INCH (10CM)-WIDE EYE SOCKETS HOUSED EYES ABOUT 3 INCHES (7.5CM) IN DIAMETER

FRONT TEETH GRIPPED AND PULLED FLESH, WHILE SIDE AND BACK TEETH TORE AND DICED THE MEAT.

PUNY YET STRONG ARMS THAT MIGHT HAVE BEEN USED TO GRIP PREY OR PUSH UP WITH IF THE BEAST FELL OVER.

DID YOU KNOW?

T. rex could run up to 12 mph (20km/h)—way slower than a car driving at top speed.

FACT FILE

MEANING OF NAME: King of the tyrant lizards

PRONOUNCED: Tie-ran-oh-sore-us

SIZE: 39 feet (12m) long, 11.5 feet (3.5m) to top of neck, 15,400 pounds (7,000kg)

DIET: Large dinosaurs, such as *Triceratops* and *Edmontosaurus*

WHEN IT LIVED: Late Cretaceous (68–66 million years ago)

DISCOVERED BY: Barnum Brown was credited with its discovery in 1902

Tyrannosaurus Rex

HOW DINOSAURS CONQUERED THE WORLD

The dinosaurs' rise to dominance was once thought to be driven by brute force. But that's far from the truth.

Text by Dr. Darren Naish, paleontologist at the University of Southampton and the author of *The Great Dinosaur Discoveries*.

The Mesozoic Era—the vast span of time that extended from 250 to 66 million years ago—is famously described as the "Age of Dinosaurs." It was once thought that these mighty reptiles were able to rule the planet due to sheer brute force alone, but a discovery made over 50 years ago of the earliest large dinosaur known, called *Herrerasaurus*, would turn this idea on its head. Subsequent fossil finds in recent years have added weight to the argument that the dinosaurs didn't out-muscle rivals to become the dominant force. Indeed, it now seems that their success was nothing more than a fluke.

Discovering how the dinosaur age got started has never been an easy task. Species from the Triassic period at the dawn of the Mesozoic have been known since the 1800s. But the creatures discovered, including the bipedal predator *Coelophysis* and the omnivorous, long-necked *Plateosaurus*, are mostly from the latest part of the Late Triassic—they are about 210 million years old. These animals are fairly large, 10 feet (3m) long or more, with sophisticated skulls that show that they are relatively advanced members of the dinosaur family tree. The lack of older, more primitive, dinosaurs long made it difficult to understand what happened during the earliest stages of their evolution.

DID YOU KNOW?

6% of terrestrial animals were dinosaurs before the extinction events of the Late Triassic.

It was the discovery of *Herrerasaurus* in 1963 that gave us a window into some of the earliest years of the dinosaurs. A team led by Argentine paleontologist Dr. Osvaldo Reig studied the remains of a surprisingly old dinosaur at Ischigualasto in northwestern Argentina. Reig named the animal *Herrerasaurus* after local farmer Victorino Herrera, who first spotted the fossils. These remains are from the earliest part of the Late Triassic, and hence are about 230 million years old. Reig knew *Herrerasaurus* was a predator of some sort, but the remains were not good enough for him to reconstruct the animal's appearance and lifestyle confidently.

> It's become clear that the earliest, timid dinosaurs did not go through a rapid evolution.

Far better specimens were discovered in 1988, when Dr. Paul Sereno at the University of Chicago and colleagues searched anew at the same spot. Thanks to these finds, we now know *Herrerasaurus* was bipedal, with a narrow snout, long, "re-curved" teeth that curve back making it hard for prey to escape, and large raking claws on the inner three fingers of its five-fingered hands. It was large, reaching 15 feet (4.5m)—roughly the length of a large car—and weighing perhaps 441 pounds (200kg). To date, *Herrerasaurus* remains the oldest large dinosaur we know of. Compared to dinosaurs from the Jurassic and Cretaceous, the two later periods within the Mesozoic, 15 feet (4.5m) is not large at all. But compared to other dinosaurs from the early part of the Late Triassic, it was a giant.

In 1991, Sereno and colleagues discovered another Ischigualasto dinosaur, later dubbed *Eoraptor*. It seems to have been a far more typical Triassic dinosaur, and indeed a variety of similarly aged species are now known. All are lightly built and less than 6.5 feet (2m) long. Most must have been omnivores, foraging in the undergrowth and keeping out of sight. The timid species discovered belong to different branches of the dinosaur family tree, so we can be sure that being small and inconspicuous was the lifestyle adopted by most early dinosaurs.

Paleontologist Dr. Paul Sereno holds a skull of *Herrerasaurus* found in Patagonia.

What If the Competitors of the Dinosaurs Had Survived?

Dinosaurs (top right) have come out on top, despite competition from croc-line archosaurs (top left) and early mammals (bottom right).

The latest evidence shows that the dinosaurs owe their rise to world domination to two extinction events at the end of the Triassic period. But what if these extinction events never occurred?

For starters, it's likely that the croc-line archosaurs would have persisted as top predators. Ironically, this means that the appearance of amphibious, freshwater crocodiles and alligators would have been prevented. The persistence of their ancestors would have left no ecological niches to fill in swamps and rivers.

Dinosaurs and other bird-line archosaurs would have continued to live in the background and would have remained small. The dominance of the croc-line archosaurs would have left few ecological niches for the dinosaurs to exploit, so many of the species we know to have existed would not have developed. Interestingly, this means that birds would not have appeared, since their origin was contingent on the diversification and success of predatory dinosaurs.

What about mammals? As in the real world, we can be confident that small burrowers, swimmers, and climbers would have evolved during the Mesozoic, and would have tried to avoid the attentions of croc-line archosaurs. The evolution of large mammals with unusual body shapes—whales, antelopes, and humans, for example—would have depended on the asteroid that killed off the dinosaurs 66 million years ago killing off croc-line archosaurs.

But, if we imagine that this extinction event at the end of the Cretaceous did finally knock the croc-line archosaurs out of the game, mammals would now have to contend with small-bodied dinosaurs. It's likely the dinosaurs—still small and inconspicuous—would have lived through the asteroid strike. Then mammals and dinosaurs would have raced to evolve a large size.

But, even if large dinosaurs had evolved, just as humans are good at extinguishing megafauna today, it's likely we would still have risen to dominate, taming and farming dinosaurs for our own ends (see page 76).

How Dinosaurs Conquered the World

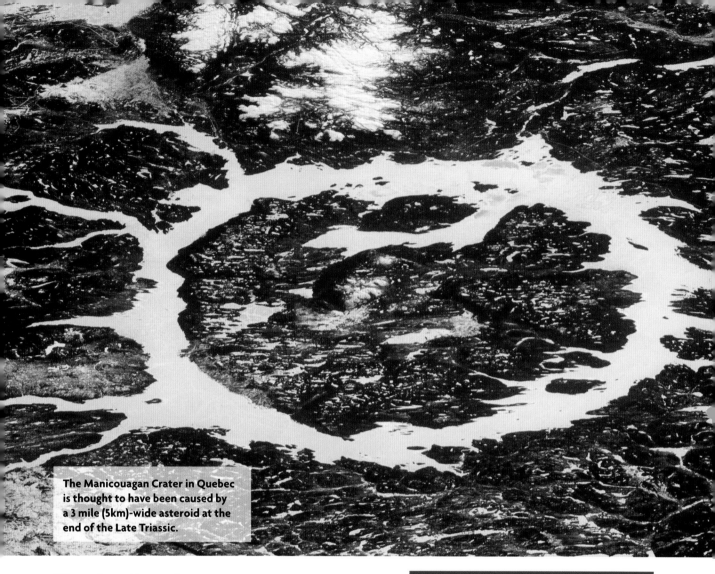

The Manicouagan Crater in Quebec is thought to have been caused by a 3 mile (5km)-wide asteroid at the end of the Late Triassic.

Three's a Crowd

These early dinosaurs were far from alone in the Triassic world. Dinosaurs are part of a major group of reptiles called *archosaurs*. Early in the Triassic, archosaurs diverged into one lineage that led to dinosaurs and later to birds, and another that led to crocodiles and their relatives. These are respectively termed "bird-line" and "croc-line" archosaurs.

Some of the croc-line archosaurs that lived in the Triassic were top predators. At more than 16 feet (5m) long, they were able to attack and defeat an animal like *Herrerasaurus*. In fact, many croc-line archosaurs evolved body shapes and lifestyles that mimicked those of the dinosaurs that would emerge more than 50 million years later.

How did dinosaurs go from being small, furtive animals of the background to a dominant force?

DID YOU KNOW?

30 million years is how long early dinosaurs remained small and inconspicuous.

Meanwhile, the ancestors of mammals—the synapsids—included small, furry, mammal-like forms as well as tusked, pig-sized herbivores and badger- and rat-sized omnivores and predators. For much of the twentieth century, it was believed that dinosaurs were competitively superior to croc-line archosaurs and synapsids. It was thought that members of these groups literally tussled for dominance on the Triassic plains, and with their long, erect legs, clawed hands and sprightly abilities, the dinosaurs were able to win the evolutionary race. Croc-line archosaurs would, so it was supposed, have had to abandon their claim on the land and eke out a living forever afterward as marsh- and lake-dwelling crocodiles and alligators.

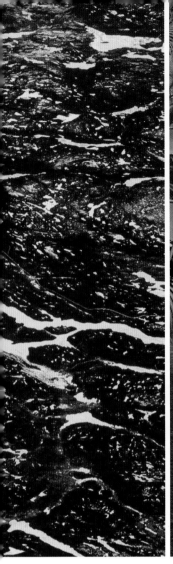

***Herrerasaurus* was one of the earliest dinosaurs. It had a sliding lower jaw— useful for snaring prey.**

But new discoveries have painted a more complex picture. Claims that dinosaurs were special compared to other archosaurs and to synapsids no longer ring true. Indeed, the earliest, timid dinosaurs did not go through a rapid evolution that would turn them into fighting machines.

Since 2003, there has been a burst of discoveries of dinosauromorph fossils—dinosauromorphs being the creatures that gave rise to the dinosaurs and lived alongside them for millions of years in the Triassic. These new fossils have shown that dinosaurs were not especially different from the dinosauromorphs. So the dinosaurs emerged quietly, without any dramatic increase in body size or important shift in lifestyle or ecology from among this group of small predators or omnivores. Looked at objectively, there is nothing in the fossil record that makes the success of dinosaurs look at all inevitable. In fact, it was a world that belonged to croc-line archosaurs. So, what happened? How did dinosaurs go from being small, furtive animals of the background to a dominant global force?

The strongest evidence appears to show that two mass extinction events—both occurring during the last part of the Triassic—removed large-bodied synapsids and croc-line archosaurs from the equation, leaving dinosaurs to rule the world.

The first of these extinctions happened about 220 million years ago. Many larger-bodied synapsids died off at this time, as did various non-dinosaurian reptile groups and numerous marine species. A climatic change, perhaps triggered by the splitting of the Pangaean supercontinent—the huge landmass that incorporated all the continents we now see—caused aridity in many areas. It has been suggested that the resultant change in vegetation and rainfall initiated a cascade of ecological consequences.

The second mass extinction event happened at the very end of the Triassic, 200 million years ago. It seems to have caused major, rapid changes to the global flora and fauna. The impact of an asteroid is a likely cause of this event, just as it is for the extinction event of 66 million years ago that wiped out the dinosaurs themselves (except for the birds, the lineage of dinosaurs that survived).

The Dinosaur vs. the Rivals

TRADITIONALLY CONSIDERED THE DOMINANT FORCE IN THE MESOZOIC, DINOSAURS WEREN'T THE BIGGEST, OR FIERCEST, PREHISTORIC HEAVYWEIGHTS.

Silesaurus ▲
(Dinosauromorph)
SIZE: 7.5 feet (2.3m) long
DIET: Leaves, buds, small animals
ATTACK AND DEFENSE: Weak bite—mostly relied on running from danger

Silesaurus and related dinosauromorphs were slender, long-limbed quadrupeds that avoided the attentions of both predatory croc-line archosaurs and early predatory dinosaurs. A small head and teeth suggest that these animals ran away from danger. Dinosauromorphs similar to *Silesaurus* gave rise to dinosaurs some time during the Middle Triassic. Fossils from the earliest-known dinosaur, *Nyasasaurus parringtoni*, date from this era.

Saurosuchus ▲
(Croc-line archosaur)
SIZE: 23 feet (7m) long
DIET: Croc-line archosaurs, dinosaurs, dinosauromorphs
ATTACK AND DEFENSE: Slashing bites taken with huge fangs and powerful jaws

Saurosuchus was one of the largest and most terrifying of the rauisuchians, a group of predatory croc-line archosaurs. Quadrupedal, erect-limbed, and probably fast and agile for its size, it would have been an arch-predator, capable of killing most animals of the time, including dinosaurs like *Herrerasaurus*. Its skull was deep but narrow, with long, curved, serrated teeth lining the jaws. Armor plates protected the top of its neck, back, and tail.

Poposaurus ▲
(Croc-line archosaur)
SIZE: 13 feet (4m) long
DIET: Smaller reptiles, including dinosauromorphs
ATTACK AND DEFENSE: Slashing bites, long fangs, ability to rear up on hind legs

Poposaurus looked like a large predatory dinosaur, but was actually a bipedal croc-line archosaur. The long-tailed, long-legged predator had short forelimbs. It was presumably a swift bipedal runner that used a deep upper jaw and long, re-curved teeth to inflict fatal damage to prey. It is one of several croc-line archosaurs that show how members of this group independently evolved the sort of body shapes seen later in dinosaurs.

◀ Eoraptor
(Dinosaur)

SIZE: 3 feet (1m) long
DIET: Leaves, buds, small animals
ATTACK AND DEFENSE: Mostly relied on speed to escape danger

Eoraptor was a typical early dinosaur. Like the dinosauromorphs that were its close relatives, it was a small, slender, long-legged omnivore that would have been in danger of being eaten by big, predatory croc-line archosaurs. Short forelimbs show that *Eoraptor* was bipedal. It had five slender digits on each "hand" with curved claws on the end of three of them. These claws could have been used in fighting as well as manipulating plants during foraging. Its jaws contained both leaf-shaped teeth as well as re-curved fangs.

Exaeretodon ▲
(Synapsid)

SIZE: 6 feet (1.8m) long
DIET: Leaves and stems of tough plants
ATTACK AND DEFENSE: Powerful bite with fangs and broad, shearing teeth; hides in burrows

Exaeretodon represents the synapsids, the hot-blooded, often furry Triassic ancestors of mammals. A short-legged, tubby-bodied animal, *Exaeretodon* used its shearing cheek teeth and powerfully muscled, broad jaws to slice up tough plant material. Curved, fang-like teeth at the front of the mouth could have been used in fighting. These animals were not speedy runners and probably dug burrows for shelter and to run to in a hurry to escape the clutches of larger, predatory animals.

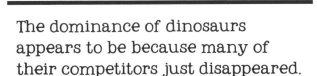

The dominance of dinosaurs appears to be because many of their competitors just disappeared.

There is even a potential "smoking gun" for this Triassic strike: the enormous Manicouagan Crater in Quebec. Representing the impact site of an object perhaps 3 miles (5km) across, it is presumably big enough to have caused major changes in the global ecosystem. Similarly aged craters in western Canada, France, the Ukraine, and North Dakota have been suggested as evidence for a series of impact events.

The Manicouagan Crater might have been formed as many as 214 million years ago. But several pieces of evidence in recent years, including a burst in fern growth, have provided support for another impact happening 200 million years ago. It's known that when other plant species are wiped out, ferns enjoy a huge growth in population. Less controversial is the massive volcanic eruption that occurred at the same time in the northern part of Pangaea. It appears to have caused global warming and ecosystem collapse.

Ruling the Roost

After these events, dinosaurs flourished—the fact that they made 50% of the tracks we now see from this time is evidence for this. Furthermore, the size of the track-makers doubles during the same period. As big animals that were living out in the open and sitting at the top of their respective food pyramids, croc-line archosaurs were presumably more adversely affected by the extinction events than the mostly small, ecologically generalized dinosaurs. The general pattern of the fossil record shows croc-line archosaurs doing okay prior to the event, but are all but absent after it.

The dominance of dinosaurs, then, appears to owe itself to the fact that many of their competitors simply disappeared. Had those extinctions not occurred, the Mesozoic could have been the age of the crocodile rather than the dinosaur. Half a century on from the discovery of *Herrerasaurus*, we know that the dinosaurs weren't as formidable a force early on as was once thought—they were fortunate survivors.

DID YOU KNOW?

75 teeth were present in the jaws of the Triassic predatory dinosaur *Herrerasaurus.*

ARCHAEOPTERYX

THE DISCOVERY OF *ARCHAEOPTERYX* IN 1861 WAS ONE OF THE MOST SIGNIFICANT AND INFLUENTIAL FOSSIL FINDS EVER MADE.

A BONY TAIL THAT IS LONG AND REPTILIAN, WITH FEATHERS SPROUTING FROM EITHER SIDE—VERY DIFFERENT FROM THE SHORT, MOSTLY FUSED TAIL OF MODERN BIRDS.

Boasting a mix of avian and reptilian characteristics, *Archaeopteryx* was a cross between a dinosaur and a bird—the crucial evolutionary missing link. Its dinosaur-like features included pointed, peg-like teeth and a long bony tail, while it also sported bird-like flight feathers and wide wings. This small carnivore was roughly the size of a raven and feasted on anything from insects to small mammals. Although there is some debate as to whether *Archaeopteryx* could take to the skies, the general consensus is that it could fly, just not very effectively, perhaps employing a range of gliding and flapping motions.

DID YOU KNOW?

Archaeopteryx is the missing link between dinosaurs and modern-day birds, which provides evidence that birds are descendants of dinosaurs.

A BRAIN SIMILAR TO THAT OF MODERN-DAY BIRDS—RELATIVELY BIG WITH ENLARGED REGIONS ASSOCIATED WITH SIGHT, SMELL, AND HEARING.

FLUFFY FLIGHT AND TAIL FEATHERS WERE CONTOURED TO PROVIDE A STREAMLINED COVERING ACROSS MUCH OF THE BODY.

PIERCING TEETH, UNLIKE MODERN BIRDS THAT INSTEAD HAVE TOOTHLESS BEAKS.

FACT FILE

MEANING OF NAME: Ancient wing

PRONOUNCED: Ark-ee-opt-er-ix

SIZE: 1.5 feet (0.5m) long, 0.75 – 1 pound (0.4 – 0.5kg)

DIET: Frogs, lizards, insects (dragonflies, beetles, mites)

WHEN IT LIVED: Late Jurassic (147 million years ago)

DISCOVERED BY: Christian Erich Hermann von Meyer in 1861

APPROXIMATE SIZE COMPARISON

Archaeopteryx

WHAT DINOSAURS LOOKED LIKE

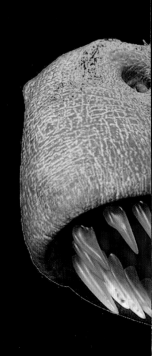

Today we take the appearance of dinosaurs for granted. It's taken centuries of careful study to learn how to accurately read the clues in the fossil records.

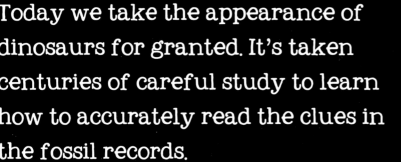

Text by John Pickrell, science journalist and author of *Flying Dinosaurs*.

The dinosaurs in Crystal Palace Park in London look quite different to how we visualize the animals today.

these kinds of reconstructions for granted these days, but just how realistic are they, and how do we know what dinosaurs really looked like?

The first attempts by humans to imagine the animals that left fossils or footprints behind were in prehistory, and there are hints that dinosaur remains made it into many ancient mythologies. Dragons appeared in Chinese texts as far back as 1100 BC, and may have been influenced by dinosaur bones. Similarly, griffins—beasts that combine an eagle with a lion—are known from ancient Greece as early as 675 BC; the inspiration may have come from fossils of the beaked dinosaur *Protoceratops*, remains of which are still found in the deserts of Central Asia today.

When ancient people were faced with strange bones, they did exactly what we do today, and used the best knowledge available to reconstruct the creatures that left them behind. Sometimes this resulted in poor conclusions. The first name assigned in print to any dinosaur remains was the ignominious title of *Scrotum humanum*—a label given by British physician Richard Brookes to the broken end of a femur in 1763, believing it to be the fossilized testicles of a biblical giant. We now know that the leg bone belonged to a *Megalosaurus*—correctly described as an extinct reptile by William Buckland in 1824. You can't entirely blame

B ack in October 2015, a new dinosaur was revealed from the 66-million-year-old Hell Creek formation in South Dakota, USA. Colorful pictures of this swift, bipedal predator—covered in feathers and with a jaw full of sharp teeth—were published around the world.

Experts behind the discovery reported that *Dakotaraptor* had large, sickle-shaped claws on the second toes of its hind feet, and would have been about 16 feet (5m) long and slightly taller than a human. This made it one of the largest ever dromaeosaurs ("swift seizers"), the group to which *Velociraptor* also belongs. We take

THE KEY EXPERIMENT

DINOSAURS WEREN'T JUST GREEN AND BLACK. RECENT RESEARCH HAS ALLOWED SCIENTISTS TO UNVEIL THE TRUE COLORS OF *SINOSAUROPTERYX*.

Back in 2010, *Sinosauropteryx* became the first dinosaur to be illustrated in its true colors. Since then, other feathered dinosaurs, like *Archaeopteryx* and *Microraptor*, have had their colors determined too.

This extraordinary detective story began with the discovery of fossilized melanosomes. These are the tiny packages of pigment inside feathers and hair in living birds and mammals, and are responsible for making your hair black, brown, blond, or ginger. These melanosomes are incredibly tough, and under the right conditions can survive hundreds of millions of years in fossils.

When you look at the feathers of a living bird under a high-powered electron microscope, you can see melanosomes of different shapes. Zebra finches have round "phaeomelanosomes" in the orange part of their feathers and sausage-shaped "eumelanosomes" in the black parts.

A team led by Mike Benton at the University of Bristol used this technique to look at the feathers along the head, neck, and back of the fossilized *Sinosauropteryx*. They found that it was ginger with white stripes down its tail and a dark band around its eyes.

***Sinosauropteryx* lived around 126 million years ago in what is now northeastern China.**

> Melanosomes are tiny packages of pigment inside feathers that give them their color.

Brookes for his conclusions, as dinosaurs would not be described as a group until 1842. That was when Richard Owen, head of what is now the Natural History Museum in London, revealed to the world a new class of strange, extinct creatures he called dinosaurs, meaning "fearfully great reptiles."

He imagined *Iguanodon*, *Megalosaurus*, and *Hylaeosaurus* to be reptiles with legs sprawled out to the sides, with scaly gray or green skin: something like modern lizards or crocodiles. In 1854 artist Benjamin Waterhouse Hawkins created life-sized sculptures of these animals as directed by Owen, and you can still see these on display in Crystal Palace Park in south London. Visit them and you will see they look very different to how we depict dinosaurs today.

Over time, we have come to completely revise our understanding of the appearance of dinosaurs, and much of this began with the description of another American dromaeosaur called *Deinonychus* in the 1960s. John Ostrom at Yale University made the revolutionary suggestion that this species was a bird-like, fast, warm-blooded pack hunter, and so began the "dinosaur renaissance" of the 1960s and 1970s. Ostrom championed the idea that birds were dinosaurs, and was spectacularly vindicated when *Sinosauropteryx*, the first known feathered dinosaur, was found in China in 1996.

When faced with new fossils today, paleontologists have a much bigger body of knowledge to draw upon when creating reconstructions. In fact, our knowledge has increased to the degree that—somewhat miraculously—we can even tell the colors of the feathers of a range of dinosaur species.

All dinosaur reconstructions begin with their fossilized bones. If paleontologists are lucky enough to have found a fairly complete skeleton, they can arrange these bones into the

Megalosaurus is described by William Buckland (pictured) as a giant reptile.

1824

1842

Richard Owen names dinosaurs as a group. Early depictions show them as giant lizards.

Giant carnivore and dinosaur-poster-boy *Tyrannosaurus rex* is named by Henry Fairfield Osborn, president of the American Museum of Natural History.

1905

1964

Deinonychus is discovered by John Ostrom, leading to the "dinosaur renaissance"—a rebirth of interest and research into the animals.

The first known feathered dinosaur, *Sinosauropteryx*, is discovered in China by a team including Canadian dinosaur hunter Philip Currie.

1996

2010

Sinosauropteryx becomes the first dinosaur to have its colors revealed, thanks to preserved melanosomes found in its fossilized feathers.

2014

New fossils allow scientists to piece together the detailed appearance of *Spinosaurus*, showing it was the largest ever carnivorous dinosaur. It was adapted to life in and out of water.

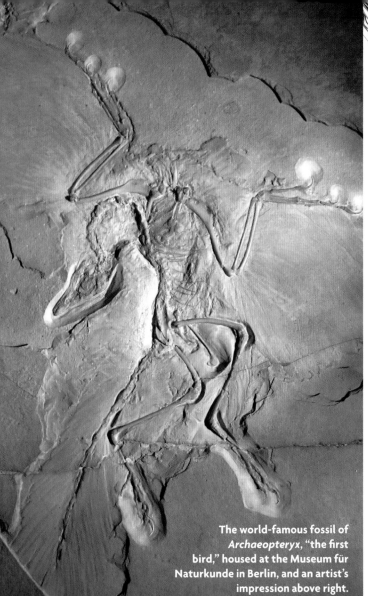

can be compared to fill in the gaps, and if there are parts of the skeletons that are still unaccounted for, experts will often look to related species of dinosaur for help with the reconstruction.

Detailed knowledge of the anatomy of a range of modern species (a field known as comparative anatomy) is helpful here, and many dinosaur experts are excellent anatomists. To those in the know, small details of the shape of bones can reveal a great deal of information about the animal they came from. For example, dinosaurs and birds (which are a kind of theropod dinosaur) are unique in having a hole in their pelvis called a "perforated acetabulum" into which the top of the thigh bone (femur) fits on each side. This is a unique trait of dinosaurs, allowing them to stand erect with their legs underneath their bodies, rather than sprawling out to the sides as in other reptiles. The dinosaur hip also allows experts to identify between the two major branches of the dinosaur family—ornithischians and saurischians.

Theropods, the carnivorous group of saurischian dinosaurs to which *T. rex*, *Allosaurus*, and now *Dakotaraptor* belong, have a series of other telltale traits in the fossils. These include hollow bones full of air pockets, three fingers on the hands, and much reduced fourth and fifth digits on the feet. Maniraptorans, the group of theropods from which birds evolved, have more distinct features, including an unusual wrist joint with a bone called a "semilunate carpal." This gave these carnivores more flexible wrists—useful for seizing prey with their hands—and allowed the flight stroke of birds to evolve.

When you're out on a dig with experts, you realize that even small details, such as the shape of teeth or the curves of limb bones, are enough for

The world-famous fossil of *Archaeopteryx*, "the first bird," housed at the Museum für Naturkunde in Berlin, and an artist's impression above right.

appropriate order—based on how the bones of birds, crocodiles, and even people are arranged—and start to get a sense of the shape of the creature.

Complete dinosaur skeletons are, however, very rare. The majority of fossil specimens have bones missing, and a great number of species are only known from a fraction of the original skeleton. In these cases, the bones of different specimens

***Ankylosaurus*'s club tail could shatter bones.**

A handful of herbivores have been found with bristles and feather-related features.

experts to make rapid assessments about the specific types of dinosaur that they belonged to.

Beyond Bones

Bones, however, are only the start of a dinosaur reconstruction. It's also important to think about muscles. For example, discs of muscle between the vertebrae of a sauropod dinosaur such as *Brachiosaurus* or *Diplodocus* would have made a great difference to the overall length of the animal. Muscles are added by referencing the exact positions and shapes of muscles in living animals. Fossilized bones often have "muscle scars" that show attachment points, which aid in this process. Since we know that larger, heavier modern animals have bigger marks, we know we need to add bigger muscles to those dinosaurs.

Our understanding of the finer details of dinosaur anatomy has altered over time, and continues to improve with 3D computer models that use the physiology of living animals to make predictions about extinct species. Paleontologists are increasingly making use of digital, biomechanical models to test their ideas about how dinosaurs walked and used their jaws.

Finally, layers of fat and skin are added to our reconstructions, as well as scales, feathers, armor, crests, and any other features such as cheeks, lips, claws, and beaks. There are surprising pieces of evidence that come to bear on these decisions too. We have some truly incredible skin impressions for a range of dinosaurs—particularly herbivores like *Edmontosaurus* and *Saurolophus*. The prevalence of scaly skin impressions in the fossils of herbivorous dinosaurs has led experts to believe that the majority had scales instead of feathers (but a handful of herbivorous dinosaurs have been found with bristles and other feather-related features).

We also know that some herbivores, particularly the armored ankylosaurs, were covered in defensive bony plates, spikes, and knobs. These bony growths in the skin, known as osteoderms, often fossilized and give a good sense of how animals like *Scelidosaurus* would have appeared in life.

In herbivorous dinosaurs, there are other features that we can infer from the bones in the skull. Duck-billed hadrosaurs have large grinding teeth at the backs of their jaws, and it's likely that these were covered with cheeks, allowing them to hold more food in their mouths for chewing before swallowing. In other dinosaurs,

such as *Protoceratops*, *Triceratops*, and *Oviraptor*, we can see the inner bony part of a beak that, in life, would likely have been covered with an outer keratinous layer as in birds today. Keratin is the same tough protein that feathers, hair, fur, and fingernails are made of. Did dinosaurs have lips? This is something we still don't know, and is an area of current debate.

Fluffy Theropods

In contrast to the herbivores, many carnivorous theropods were probably covered in feathers. The incredible fossils of nearly 50 species—mostly from China's northeastern province of Liaoning—show a range of feathery coverings, from downy, insulating "dino-fuzz" to flashy display and flight feathers. Some of these animals are so exquisitely preserved that we can see the shape and arrangement of feathers right across their bodies.

Though most of these feathered dinosaurs have been found in China, the spread of species across the family tree suggests that many theropods in other parts of the world were feathered too—we just have a fantastic window into the past with Liaoning because of the type of preservation found in its volcanic deposits.

Sometimes we have other evidence of feathers, such as marks on the forearm bones of *Velociraptor*, which correlate to the "quill knobs" where the ligaments of flight feathers attach on pigeons today. It's this feature in *Velociraptor* fossils from Mongolia that led experts to assume all dromaeosaurs had small "wings" on

Fossils of *Epidexipteryx* show that it may have used its feather as a display to attract mates.

NEED TO KNOW

A QUICK GLOSSARY OF KEY TERMS USED IN DINOSAUR APPEARANCE

COMPARATIVE ANATOMY

The study of similarities and differences in the physical features of various species. This allows experts to make informed guesses about the appearance of extinct species based on living animals.

MELANOSOMES

These tiny granules of pigment are responsible for the coloring of hair and feathers in animals and birds. Preserved melanosomes in a *Sinosauropteryx* fossil revealed this dinosaur's true colors.

PALEONTOLOGY

The study of prehistoric life, based on the fossils of animals, plants and other organisms, as well as the ages and details of the layers of rock they were found in.

THEROPOD

This large group of bipedal and mostly carnivorous dinosaurs includes *T. rex*, *Allosaurus* and *Sinosauropteryx*. The first birds evolved from theropods around 150 million years ago.

Feathers evolved for another purpose entirely and were only later co-opted for flight.

their forearms—a feature now confirmed by the Chinese fossil of another new dromaeosaur called *Zhenyuanlong*. Quill knobs were also found in the *Dakotaraptor* fossil. The scientists behind this discovery estimated it to have had a wingspan of around 3 feet (1m).

But, in the years following the discovery of *Sinosauropteryx* in 1996, it became clear that most carnivorous theropods wouldn't have been able to fly—they didn't have fully formed wings or they weren't the right kind of shape. Paleontologists began to realize that feathers evolved for another purpose entirely and were only later co-opted for flight.

The feathers of many of these animals were simpler in structure than anything we'd recognize as feathers today, and it's likely

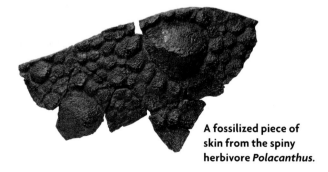

A fossilized piece of skin from the spiny herbivore *Polacanthus*.

Mark Norell at the American Museum of Natural History studies whether dinosaurs used feathers for displays.

they were used like the downy fuzz of chicks for insulation. "To start with, feather structures are not all that complicated—they are a coat of simple filaments," says Dr. Paul Barrett, a paleontologist at the Natural History Museum in London. "These animals are small and quite active, they have elevated metabolic rates . . . and this is a way of retaining heat."

After feathers first found a use in insulation, they developed another purpose. In 2007, in Inner Mongolia, Chinese Academy of Science experts unearthed the fossil of a bird-of-paradise-sized dinosaur, which they called *Epidexipteryx*, Greek for "display feather." These scientists noted in a 2008 *Nature* article: "Ornamental plumage is used to send signals essential to a wide range of avian behavior patterns, particularly relating to courtship. It is highly probable that the [tail feathers] of *Epidexipteryx* had display as their primary function."

The fossilized creature retained traces of four, long, ribbon-like feathers, which it could have flicked and wafted as it danced to woo mates, as birds of paradise do today. This weird dinosaur was a compelling piece of evidence that early feathers were used for display too.

Other groups of dinosaurs had big "pennaceous" feathers (with a central vane and interlocking barbs running off to either side) on their forearms and tails, which were more obviously used for showing off.

A 2013 study by experts including Phil Currie and Scott Persons at the University of Alberta, and Mark Norell at the American Museum of Natural History, provides perhaps the best evidence yet that dinosaurs used feathers for elaborate displays. Oviraptorids are parrot-beaked omnivorous theropods that had a "pygostyle" tail, where the final few vertebrae are fused to form a ridged, blade-like structure. The researchers found marks on the bones of five different species of oviraptorids, which suggested

large muscles that would have allowed the stumpy tail to be flexed and posed in a number of ways. The conclusion was that male oviraptorids likely indulged in tail-shaking mating displays, much as turkeys and peacocks do today.

So there's good evidence of early feathers being used for insulation and display, but how did they come to find a function in flight? Eventually, the extra surface area of feathers on the tail and forearms used for display would have offered some lift when jumping or gliding. Then evolution would have started to select for the running or flying functions of feathers, eventually leading to four-winged dinosaurs such as *Changyuraptor* and *Microraptor* that lived in the trees.

Despite the fact that paleontologists think many carnivorous theropods were covered in feathers, until recently, the consensus was that *T. rex* and other large theropods probably only had feathers as juveniles, if at all. The idea was that huge animals don't need insulation, as they lose heat to the environment very slowly. But the discovery of a series of feathered relatives of *Tyrannosaurus* has turned this idea on its head. The first, *Dilong paradoxus*, was discovered by legendary dinosaur hunter Professor Xing Xu in Liaoning in 2004. As this lightly built, 125 million-year-old

KNOWN TYPES OF DINOSAUR FEATHERS

Sinosauropteryx

Caudipteryx

Anchiornis

Archaeopteryx

Confuciusornis

Yutyrannus huali had downy feathers over much of its body.

predator was relatively small, at 6.5 feet (2m) in length, its downy covering was not wholly unexpected.

Much more surprising, though, was the 29.5 foot (9m)-high *Yutyrannus huali* discovered in 2012. Also from the Early Cretaceous deposits of Liaoning, this shaggy predator was closer in size to *T. rex* itself. It showed that downy feathers were probably more widespread among dinosaurs than anyone had expected. *Yutyrannus* is the largest feathered animal ever known to have lived.

A few of the new fossils, however, hint that feathers might have originated much deeper in the dinosaur family tree, not close to the ancestors of modern birds. For example, *Tianyulong confuciusi* was a small bipedal herbivore with a fuzzy covering of fluff. Nothing unusual in that, except it's in the ornithischian group of herbivorous dinosaurs, which are very distant cousins to the carnivorous theropods. Another ornithischian—*Psittacosaurus*, a small and early relative of *Triceratops*—also had bristle-like

structures, which may have been a form of feather. And the Siberian species, *Kulindadromeus zabaikalicus*, is the best evidence so far that feathers may have been very widespread across all dinosaur groups. This 5 foot (1.5m)-long ornithischian herbivore may have had three different types of feathery filament, and scales on different parts of its body.

Flying Reptiles

There's even the tantalizing possibility that feathers originated in the ancestors of animals that gave rise to dinosaurs and their sister group of flying reptiles, the pterosaurs. "Even the filaments of pterosaurs are likely to be a kind of primitive feather," argues Xu, a world expert on feathered dinosaurs at the Institute for Vertebrate Paleontology in Beijing. Experts have known for some years that many pterosaurs had a fur-like covering, which perhaps helped them maintain a high metabolic rate for flight, but it's not yet clear if this is related to feathers or evolved independently.

Others aren't so sure that feathers were common across all dinosaur groups. There's no evidence of feathers in most other ornithischians, according to a 2013 study by David Evans of the Royal Ontario Museum and Paul Barrett. "We have lots of skin impressions from duck-billed and horned dinosaurs, and none of them show anything that looks like feathers," says Barrett. This could be because the ancestors of these dinosaurs started off with feathers and lost them, or it could just be that dinosaurs

CAST OF CHARACTERS

SIX INNOVATIVE SCIENTISTS WHO HELPED US DECIPHER WHAT DINOSAURS LOOKED LIKE

Richard Owen (1804–1892) Was head of what is now the Natural History Museum in London. He was an influential anatomist and paleontologist who described dinosaurs as a group. He reconstructed a series of the earliest known species, including *Megalosaurus*, *Iguanodon*, and *Hylaeosaurus*.

John Ostrom (1928–2005) Discovered and described *Deinonychus*— hailed as one of the most important fossil finds. He reconstructed it as a warm-blooded, speedy predator—at odds with the idea of slow, lumbering dinosaurs. He brought back the idea that birds evolved from dinosaurs.

Robert T. Bakker (1945–) Was a student of John Ostrom. Bakker went on to lead the charge of the "dinosaur renaissance," theorizing on physiology and locomotion and suggesting that, unlike modern lizards, dinosaurs were warm-blooded. The jury is still out on this.

have within their genes the mechanism to easily evolve skin-related structures, he says. "They also have lots of armor and spikes that form in the skin too." It could explain why some groups have feathers, frills, or armor and others don't.

The question now is did all dinosaurs and pterosaurs inherit feathers from the same common ancestor, or is it just that the group had a remarkable plasticity to play around with different structures like bristles, quills, fuzz, fluff, ribbons, and, eventually, complex and beautiful feathers sculpted for the purpose of flight? Research is ongoing, so hopefully we'll soon know more.

Prehistoric Palette

In the meantime, artists play an essential role in bringing dinosaurs to life, and often have expert anatomical and paleontological knowledge to build on the scientific evidence with informed guesswork. Without these paleoillustrators, the appearance of these animals would live only inside the minds of the scientists who discovered them.

In the last five years or so, the colors of dinosaur feathers have come into focus, but we may soon have a good idea of dinosaur skin colors too. We already know from the patterns of scales on some "mummified" fossils that *Edmontosaurus* was probably adorned with stripy patterns, and a number of studies have

Microraptor is thought to have had feathers like this.

Recent studies have shown that the four-winged *Microraptor* had iridescent plumage.

started to use electron microscopes to look at the structural patterns of tiny packages of pigment in the skin. In 2015, an international team of scientists used this technique to show that a prehistoric marine reptile called a mosasaur had a dark back and a pale-colored belly. It won't be long before similar methods are used to determine the colors of dinosaurs too.

Reconstructing animals from fossils is partly guesswork, but it's informed guesswork, building on the knowledge built up over the centuries. Today, we have a better idea of the appearance of dinosaurs than ever before.

Gregory S. Paul
(1954–)
Is an artist and paleontologist whose books and anatomically accurate dinosaur illustrations have inspired a generation of artists and many of the dinosaur illustrations you see today. His work pioneered the revised look of dinosaurs in the 1970s.

Mike Benton
(1956–)
Is a paleontologist at the University of Bristol. He led a team of researchers in 2010 to determine the color of dinosaurs. They showed that *Sinosauropteryx* was covered in fluffy ginger and white feathers.

Xu Xing
(1956–)
Has discovered more dinosaurs than just about anyone else alive today. These include more than half of the feathered dinosaurs found in China.

ANKYLOSAURUS

WITH ITS THICK LAYERS OF ARMOR AND SOLID, CLUBBED TAIL POWERFUL ENOUGH TO SHATTER BONES, *ANKYLOSAURUS* WAS TOUGHER THAN ANY ARMY TANK.

Its outer layer of skin was reinforced with bones called osteoderms, forming an impenetrable sheet of armor, a feature shared with modern-day crocodiles. But most predators wouldn't even manage to reach its robust body because of the deadly swinging club at the end of its tail. With this arsenal of weaponry, you might expect *Ankylosaurus* to be a formidable predator; however, it was actually a herbivore, using its artillery for defense. *Ankylosaurus* had numerous leaf-shaped teeth at the back of its jaws, but the front of the mouth was toothless and equipped with a horny beak to pluck plants from the undergrowth. It may have digested the plant matter via fermentation, the same process used to produce alcohol.

BROAD BEAK FOR CONSUMING MOUTHFULS OF LOW-GROWING HERBS AND OTHER PLANTS.

STRONG SENSE OF SMELL LARGELY DUE TO AN AREA OF THE BRAIN DEVOTED TO SMELL (OLFACTORY BULB).

APPROXIMATE SIZE COMPARISON

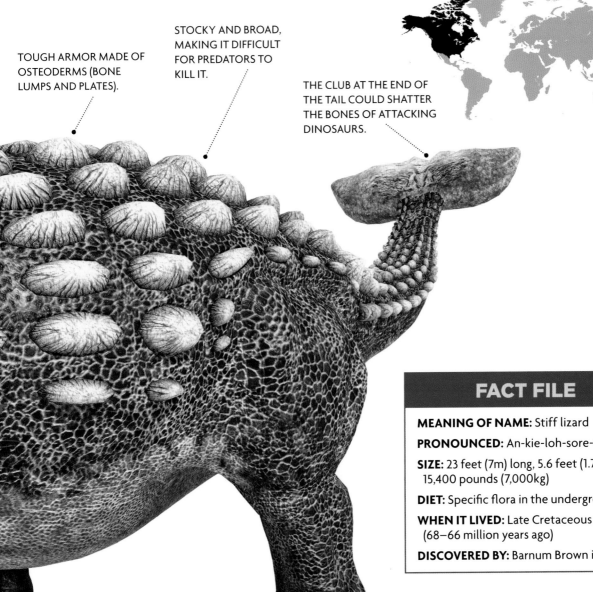

TOUGH ARMOR MADE OF OSTEODERMS (BONE LUMPS AND PLATES).

STOCKY AND BROAD, MAKING IT DIFFICULT FOR PREDATORS TO KILL IT.

THE CLUB AT THE END OF THE TAIL COULD SHATTER THE BONES OF ATTACKING DINOSAURS.

FACT FILE

MEANING OF NAME: Stiff lizard

PRONOUNCED: An-kie-loh-sore-us

SIZE: 23 feet (7m) long, 5.6 feet (1.7m) tall, 15,400 pounds (7,000kg)

DIET: Specific flora in the undergrowth

WHEN IT LIVED: Late Cretaceous (68–66 million years ago)

DISCOVERED BY: Barnum Brown in 1906

DID YOU KNOW?

70% of all *Ankylosaurs* that have been discovered were fossilized upside down, because the floating, lifeless bodies overturned before sinking to the sea floor.

Ankylosaurus

THE DINOSAURS AMONG US

Velociraptor walked like a chicken, *T. rex* didn't roar open-mouthed, and herbivorous hadrosaurs also snacked on lobster. New research on living species is revealing the surprising lives of dinosaurs.

Text by Dr. Darren Naish, a paleontologist at the University of Southampton and the author of *The Great Dinosaur Discoveries.*

How fast—or slow—was *T. rex*? How did *Spinosaurus* catch its prey? Did the gigantic sauropods crane their necks upwards to feed from trees, or bend down to reach food on the ground? Paleontology—the study of ancient life—has more than its fair share of questions, and this is especially true when it comes to dinosaurs.

There exists no single, specific technique that allows scientists to answer questions on the biology and behavior of extinct animals. Instead, numerous different methods are employed. These include the examination of internal structure via microscopes, x-rays, and CT-scanners; the identification of scars left by muscles and wear marks caused by contact with food; the study of stomach contents, droppings, footprints, and nests; and the creation of real-world models, calculations, and 3D digital models that replicate an animal's range of movement. Many of these techniques use cutting-edge tech and software.

There is one overarching technique that guides our views on dinosaur biology. This technique is the use of analogy: the practice in which the bodies and body parts of extinct animals are compared to those of living animals.

Data on the musculature and organs of living animals are the foundation for our thoughts on dinosaur anatomy. The walking, running, and flying styles of modern reptiles, birds, and mammals are crucial to ideas on the locomotion of extinct animals. And the way the teeth, jaws, and claws of modern species are used serve as analogies for fossil species with similar adaptations.

Questions about extinct dinosaurs—about how fast they could move, how flexible their necks were, or how big their muscles were, for example—have encouraged paleontologists to look at form and function in living animals. But what happens all too frequently is that paleontologists then discover that the required studies have never been done. So, inspired by questions they have about dinosaurs, paleontologists often get involved in the requisite studies on living animals. Work on the locomotion and running speeds of elephants, neck flexibility in giraffes and big birds, and bite strength in crocodiles and alligators are all linked to studies on dinosaur form and function.

When using living animals as analogies of extinct ones, paleontologists limit the species they are analyzing using a technique called "phylogenetic bracketing," often just shortened to "bracketing." The key requirement for bracketing is a good understanding of the evolutionary tree to which the extinct animal belongs, and the existence of living animals that surround—or "bracket"—the extinct species of interest. The result is that, should we wish to know about any aspect of dinosaur biology or anatomy not preserved in fossils, we can look at the condition in those modern relatives.

Using this logic, we can make inferences about many aspects of dinosaur biology that are not yet illuminated by fossil evidence. Topics such as dinosaur mating behavior and the form of their sexual organs, the anatomy of the dinosaurian digestive system, and the nature of dinosaur eyes and visual abilities have all been studied using bracketing.

Over time, more and more of our questions about long-dead animals will be answered, both because we will find more fossils, and because new analytic techniques will improve our ability to arrive at precise answers. We will never have all the information we might like. So, extrapolation and theorizing based on analogy will always be an important part of paleontological investigation.

THE SICKLE-CLAW

HOW *VELOCIRAPTOR* USED A LARGE TALON TO PIN DOWN PREY LIKE A HAWK

Theropods often had claws that were large, pointed, strongly curved, and flattened from side-to-side. In dromaeosaurids (the theropod family that includes *Velociraptor*), the second toe was held raised up off the ground and was tipped with an especially big, curved talon, called the "sickle-claw."

Pity the prey that were pinned down by the enormous talons of *Velociraptor*.

This remarkable structure was discovered in the 1960s and initially stumped paleontologists as to its use and function. The most popular suggestion used to be that it sliced or disemboweled, and that the creature would stand on one leg and kick at the belly of a prey animal with the other—a technique not used by any modern predator. But that idea has since been turned on its head. To better understand claw function in dromaeosaurids, a team led by Denver Fowler examined how owls, falcons, hawks, and eagles use them. (Surprisingly, biologists had not previously done this work.) By comparing dromaeosaurid feet with those of predatory birds, Fowler and colleagues concluded that dromaeosaurids mostly used the sickle-claw to pin prey to the ground before attacking it with the mouth.

So it seems that *Velociraptor* behaved like a giant, ground-running hawk.

Here, we take a look at the latest research on living species that is opening our eyes to the secret lives of the dinosaurs.

Zip It

How Hollywood got it wrong about the noises dinosaurs made

Paleontologists have yet to discover the remains of a dinosaur where the parts of the body associated with noise-making have been preserved. So they use bracketing to make inferences about these structures. Crocodylians and birds possess an organ in the throat called the larynx, so dinosaurs would almost certainly have had one too. Crocodylians generate sound in the larynx while birds have switched to the use of a new structure—the syrinx—located deep inside the chest. What seems likely is that dinosaurs generated sound in the larynx and that the syrinx only evolved in the lineage leading to birds.

Can we go further, and use bracketing to predict what sounds dinosaurs made? And can we use analogy to work out how they released sounds into the environment? Crocodylians and giant birds (like cassowaries and emus) make deep, rumbling sounds. These emanate across the environment as the animal exposes and inflates its neck or the front of its chest. The sounds do not emerge from the mouth. In fact, it is kept closed while the sounds are being made. So, the idea beloved of Hollywood—that dinosaurs roared with a wide-open mouth—is highly unlikely.

CT-scans of the skull of *Neovenator* (bottom right) reveal large, branching canals, suggesting they had facial nerves like those of crocs.

A SOFT TOUCH

THE SENSITIVE FACES OF CROCS AND BIRDS REVEAL CLUES TO DINOSAUR BEHAVIOR

Tiny, bony channels and canals preserved in and on some dinosaur skulls look like the structures that house sensitive facial nerves in living crocodylians and birds. CT-scans have shown that at least some theropods (perhaps most or even all of them) possess large, branching canals deep within the bones of the face. These are similar to bony channels that—in modern birds and crocodylians—house enlarged facial nerves, and give these modern animals enhanced sensitivity in the face. Might the same have been true of these in dinosaurs as well?

In a 2017 study, Chris Barker and colleagues at the University of Southampton collected data on the size and shape of the bony canals in the facial bones of the theropod *Neovenator*, a distant cousin of the more famous *Allosaurus*. They suggested that these facial canals probably did, indeed, house enlarged and complex nerves just like those of modern crocodylians, and hence that *Neovenator* had a particularly sensitive face. Crocodylians use facial sensitivity to detect the nearby movement of prey and sense temperature in their nest material, and they even rub faces during courtship. Perhaps theropods like *Neovenator* did likewise, using facial sensitivity in prey detection, nest-building, and communication.

Show-Offs
How dinosaurs attracted mates and fended off rivals

Numerous elaborate structures decorated the heads and bodies of many dinosaurs, including horns, frills, bony crests, spikes, spines, and tall sails. These structures are so odd that they were once thought to serve unusual functions. The hollow head-crests of duckbilled dinosaurs, for example, were suggested to function as air-storage tanks or snorkels used in swimming. The bony plates of stegosaurs and the dorsal frill of *Spinosaurus* were argued to be for collecting or dumping heat. The horned dinosaur frill was thought to be a special anti-predator shield, and so on.

During the late twentieth century, it became increasingly clear that analogy was a powerful tool for the interpretation of dinosaur biology. Dinosaurs were weird, but not so weird that they seem to have been doing things in a different fashion from living animals. Plus, the fact that birds are now seen as living dinosaurs means that structures shared by dinosaurs and birds alike should be imagined as similar in function.

With analogy in mind, what might we conclude as to the elaborate structures of dinosaurs? Duckbill head crests are similar to crests present in cassowaries, hornbills, and other birds. The frills and horns of ceratopsians look like the structures present in certain chameleons and other lizards. And the sail of *Spinosaurus* has an analogy in the tall frills seen on various chameleons and other members of the iguana lineage.

So far as we can tell, in modern species all these various crests, horns, frills, and sails are involved in visual display, most typically to attract mates and deter rivals. Their evolution has been driven by sexual selection, and they have important roles in breeding success.

So far, paleontologists think the elaborate structures of dinosaurs evolved within the context of sexual selection as well. Like the analogous structures of living animals, they grew far faster than the overall growth rate of the animal itself, became large and obvious only once the animal approached sexual maturity, and were costly to the animal's overall survival. Based on this evidence, it seems that the elaborate, crested, and frill-bearing dinosaurs of the past behaved in similar ways to rutting deer and displaying birds today.

A WALK IN THE JURASSIC PARK

CHICKENS AND OSTRICHES SHOW HOW DINOSAURS PROBABLY MOVED

Many quadrupedal dinosaurs—like sauropods and horned dinosaurs—have limb bones and proportions quite different from those of living animals. Tracks and articulated skeletons give us some indication of how they walked and ran. Based on analogy, it has been proposed that they were similar to elephants, rhinos, or erect-walking crocodylians. But, of course, controversy and uncertainty remains.

Extinct theropods were built much like the birds that are their descendants. Numerous studies have looked at leg structure and movement in ostriches, emus, chickens, and guinea fowl in order to better understand gait and locomotion in the extinct species.

But modern birds are different from theropods like *T. rex* and *Velociraptor* in having a substantially shortened tail, wider hips, and in doing more of their leg movement at the knee rather than the hip. In an effort to compensate for these differences and better understand locomotion in ancient, long-tailed theropods, Bruno Grossi and colleagues actually raised chickens with a long, tail-like prosthesis attached to their rear ends. These birds learned to walk with a more "dinosaur-like" gait, thus proving that birds still have this ability if aspects of their proportions undergo change.

A Bite to Eat
Modern-day crocs reveal how carnivorous dinosaurs feasted

A critical component of feeding behavior is bite strength, since it shows which food items an animal is adapted for. It wasn't until the 1990s, however, that tools and data allowed paleontologists to make refined estimates of dinosaur bite strength, and compare them with those of living animals. In general, these comparisons confirm expectations. The crocodile-faced spinosaurs, for example, have skulls where pressure is conducted across the bones just as it is in the bones of robust-skulled crocodylians today. This suggests that spinosaurs ate similar prey to crocodylians and handled them in the same fashion. Meanwhile, *T. rex* had a bite strength exceeding that of alligators, meaning that it could cripple prey and even break bones.

Food Fermenters
The dinosaurs that digested food like herbivorous birds and reptiles today

The guts of dinosaurs have—in virtually all cases—long since rotted away. So what do living animals tell us about them? Using the bracketing technique, we can infer that dinosaurs had an esophagus, a bag-like stomach, and an intestine that ended with a cloaca. The fact that many herbivorous dinosaurs had broad, massive bodies and ate fibrous plant material suggests, by analogy with modern herbivorous birds and reptiles, that they were hindgut fermenters—that most digestion occurred slowly in the intestines, and that those intestines were long and voluminous.

Herbivores, such as *Iguanodon*, probably had long intestines.

Cheating Vegetarians

How some herbivorous dinosaurs snacked on meat

Herbivory was widespread in dinosaurs. Many species would have spent much of their time finding and consuming leaves, shoots, and fruit, as shown by their jaws, teeth, and bodies. But if we look at the modern analogies of herbivorous dinosaurs—reptiles like iguanas and tortoises, birds like grouse, and mammals like deer and antelopes—we see that even dedicated herbivores are not as strict as conventionally thought.

Modern plant eaters of all sorts sometimes snack on animals. Cattle, deer, and other hoofed mammals eat baby birds, eggs, and small mammals on occasion, and plant-eating lizards, tortoises, and birds pick at carcasses and swallow small animals if they can. Some of this occasional carnivory results from dietary deficiency. Mammals like deer require large quantities of calcium to grow antlers, and the eating of bony animals gives them the minerals they crave.

In recent years, paleontologists have come to believe that herbivorous dinosaurs were occasionally carnivorous. Many likely required extra calcium to fuel their growth, and had teeth and jaws suited for chewing on animal matter.

Evidence for this finally surfaced recently with the discovery of crustacean shells in the fossilized dung of duckbilled hadrosaurs.

TRICERATOPS

DESPITE ITS INTIMIDATING "THREE-HORNED FACE" AND HEFTY 12,000-POUND (5,500-KG) BODY, *TRICERATOPS* FELL PREY TO THE MIGHTY *TYRANNOSAURUS REX*.

ITS BODY WAS THE SIZE OF AN ELEPHANT, MAKING IT THE LARGEST HORNED DINOSAUR.

The two enormous horns protruding from above its eyes and smaller horn from its nose gave *Triceratops* its name—"three-horned face." But the beast also had a number of pointed bones jutting out from the enormous bony frill that crowned its head. All these weapons were used to battle for mates, like stags when they rut, but also to defend against predators such as ferocious *T. rex*. The bony frill was probably also used to impress potential mates. *Triceratops* had a powerful yet toothless beak. At the back of its jaws were great batteries of interlocking, diamond-shaped teeth for rasping and shearing.

APPROXIMATE SIZE COMPARISON

DID YOU KNOW?

Triceratops had a staggering 800 sharp teeth assembled in groups named batteries, which were continuously replaced.

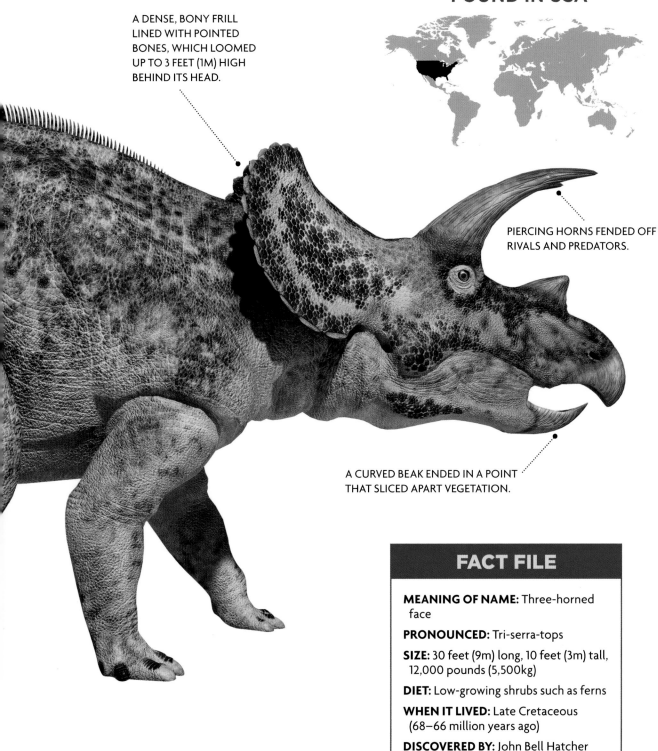

A DENSE, BONY FRILL LINED WITH POINTED BONES, WHICH LOOMED UP TO 3 FEET (1M) HIGH BEHIND ITS HEAD.

PIERCING HORNS FENDED OFF RIVALS AND PREDATORS.

A CURVED BEAK ENDED IN A POINT THAT SLICED APART VEGETATION.

FACT FILE

MEANING OF NAME: Three-horned face

PRONOUNCED: Tri-serra-tops

SIZE: 30 feet (9m) long, 10 feet (3m) tall, 12,000 pounds (5,500kg)

DIET: Low-growing shrubs such as ferns

WHEN IT LIVED: Late Cretaceous (68–66 million years ago)

DISCOVERED BY: John Bell Hatcher in 1888

Triceratops

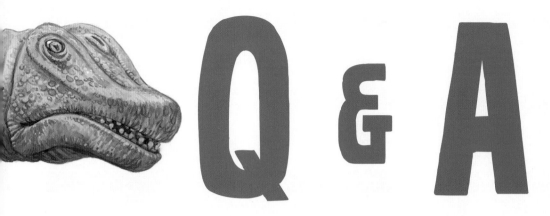

Q & A

All those dinosaur questions that you've often wondered about, but never got around to finding the answers to ...

At Their Peak, How Many Dinosaurs Roamed Earth?

There could have been around 1,800 different genera of dinosaurs. We can't directly measure the size of populations because we don't know what percentage of individuals is preserved in the fossil record. Twenty million bison roamed America in the 18th century, and dinosaurs, being egg layers, could have reproduced faster. Assuming that the availability of plants was the limiting factor, large dinosaurs probably reached comparable population sizes in the Jurassic, 150 million years ago.

Scientists estimate over 20 million dinosaurs might have roamed Earth at any one time.

What Dinosaur Was Found Most Recently?

***Matheronodon provincialis* lived in the Late Cretaceous.**

About 50 new dinosaur species are discovered every year, so that's roughly one a week. By 2017, the most recent discovery was *Matheronodon provincialis*. Discovered in October 2017 in the south of France, the herbivore chewed foliage using 2.4 inch (6cm)-long teeth adapted to produce a powerful shearing action, resembling a pair of scissors.

DID YOU KNOW?

Paleontologists have learned more about dinosaur behavior from footprint trace fossils than from actual dinosaur body fossils.

Did Earth's Previous Faster Spin Rate Make Dinosaurs Lighter?

Studies of daily growth patterns in fossilized coral and mollusks suggest that around 100 million years ago a day was about 23 hours long. That means the Earth was spinning around 5% faster, boosting the weight-reducing centrifugal effect by around 10% compared to today. Could this explain dinosaurs' huge size? No—the centrifugal effect was still far smaller than gravity's strength, and would have had a negligible effect on the weight of *T. rex* and company.

IN NUMBERS

423
Million years since the first dinosaurs graced our plant

1999
The year *Microraptor* was discovered in China—evidence of a four-winged dinosaur

How Did Dinosaurs Grow So Big?
Size does matter—but being too large can also be an issue

For many animals, there was an intrinsic selective pressure in favor of increasing body size. Since you must share your evolutionary niche with the other members of your species, being slightly larger than your peers helps you eat the higher leaves, catch bigger prey, and defend a larger territory. Even more importantly, the larger you are, the safer you are from predators.

Over time, this selective pressure has caused many animal lineages to gradually increase in size. About two years ago, scientists in South Africa reported evidence that dinosaurs became larger as they switched from walking on two legs to four.

But being large also means you need more food, can't escape from natural disasters so easily, and reproduce more slowly. As such, the fossil record is littered with examples of animals that slowly increased in size before going abruptly extinct.

The countershading across the body of *Sinosauropteryx* helped it avoid detection.

Did Any Dinosaurs Use Camouflage to Hide from Predators and Prey?

Yes. Researchers from the University of Bristol have recently revealed that the small-feathered dinosaur *Sinosauropteryx* used its color patterning to avoid being detected by predators and prey. The results suggest that it had multiple types of camouflage, including a striped tail and a dark stripe around its eyes. In modern birds, this bandit-like mask helps to hide their eyes from would-be predators. As the countershading went from dark to light high on the body, it's likely *Sinosauropteryx* lived in open habitats with little vegetation.

Why Don't Museums Have Fossils of All Species from Evolutionary History?

Every animal belongs to a species, and every species evolved from another one. It therefore follows that every fossil is of a species that is either at the end of its branch in the evolutionary tree, or is an intermediate form between one species and another. The fact that we don't always have the complete sequence of intermediate forms is because the fossil record is incomplete. But the dinosaurs, for example, evolved from a group of reptiles represented today by crocodiles, and the dinosaurs themselves evolved into modern-day birds. So, it's an oversimplification, but you could say that *T. rex* fossils are an intermediate step between a crocodile and a chicken.

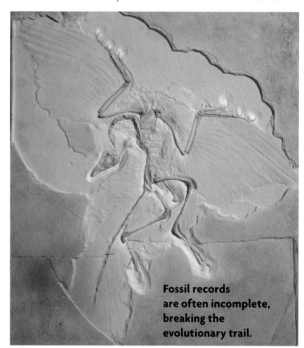

Fossil records are often incomplete, breaking the evolutionary trail.

Argentinosaurus held a number of world records.

DID YOU KNOW?

Argentinosaurus holds a number of records. It was the longest known dinosaur at a whopping 115 feet (35m), and is thought to have been the heaviest dinosaur, weighing in at an estimated 170,000 pounds (77,000kg).

Why Didn't Dinosaurs Evolve to Be More Intelligent?

They did! Dinosaurs evolved into modern birds and some of them are extremely intelligent. In Japan, there are crows that have learned to use the traffic to crack the shells of nuts that they drop—and they wait for the lights to turn red, so they can safely retrieve them.

One reason that birds still aren't as intelligent as humans is that a heavy, energy-hungry brain doesn't mix well with birds' main adaptive advantage—flying. It's important to realize that intelligence isn't the goal of evolution, nor is it always the best adaptation to the environment. The enormous sauropod dinosaurs lasted on the planet for 100 million years, despite their tiny brains. We've had "intelligence" for just a few million years, so it's too early to say whether it is a better strategy.

Archaeopteryx was an animal that shared features of both dinosaurs and modern birds.

How Are Dinosaurs Grouped?

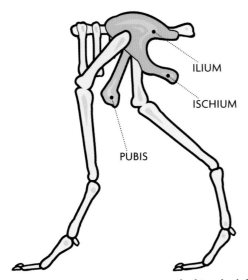

SAURISCHIA

ILIUM

ISCHIUM

PUBIS

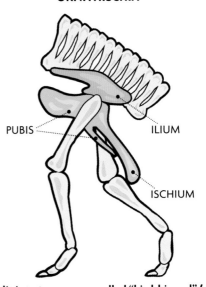

ORNITHISCHIA

PUBIS

ILIUM

ISCHIUM

The hips don't lie: dinosaurs are split into two groups, called "bird-hipped" (right) and "lizard-hipped" (left).

Broadly speaking, there are two major branches of the dinosaur family tree—split according to the pelvis shape. Saurischia, or "lizard-hipped" dinosaurs, have a pubis bone that points forward; the Ornithischia ("bird-hipped") have a backwards-pointing pubis. Any fossil with either of these pelvis types is classified as a dinosaur. Ironically, birds are actually descended from the Saurischia. Their bird hips evolved independently, much later in time.

Q & A

Where in the World Are Most Fossils Found?

Deserts are prime fossil territory, with hot spots in the United States, China, and Argentina.

Incredibly, about three-quarters of all known dinosaur species have only been found in the last 20 years, since the release of the original *Jurassic Park*. With 50% unveiled in the last 10 years alone, a new dinosaur species is crowned roughly every week.

Despite their rapid and widespread excavation, a rough estimate of the current number of dinosaur species found totals 500 of a possible 1,800 or so. This implies the exciting prospect that more dinosaur species are still hiding underground than all the species already identified.

Apatosaurus lived around 150 million years ago.

What Was the Life Expectancy of a Dinosaur?

Scientists can measure the age of some dinosaur species from the growth rings inside fossil bones, like you can tell the age of a tree by the rings inside its trunk. Using this method, the oldest known *T. rex* specimen was 28 when it died.

But this technique doesn't work well on many species, because their bones grew continuously and don't have neat growth rings. Early estimates of 300-year lifespans for the largest sauropods were based on comparisons with crocs and turtles, which have slower metabolisms. The consensus is now that *Apatosaurus* and *Diplodocus* only lived for 70 or 80 years—about the same as an elephant today.

Chinese paleontologist Dr. Xu Xing poses among the remains of duck-billed dinosaurs in Zhucheng, China.

Could We Ever Clone a Dinosaur?

The oldest DNA fragments recovered are around 800,000 years old, so dinosaur cloning is probably impossible. True cloning also requires an intact, living cell, and it has only ever been successful using a host animal of the same species. That rules out mammoth cloning too.

What we might be able to do is splice some mammoth genes into the DNA of the Asian elephant, their closest relative. Most of the mammoth genome has already been sequenced from fragments recovered from mammoths frozen in permafrost. In 2015, a team at Harvard managed to insert 14 mammoth genes into an elephant cell in a petri dish. But Asian elephants and mammoths are thought to differ by at least 400 genes, and figuring out exactly which ones are different will take a while. And then that single cell still needs to develop into an embryo and then a baby mammoth. We don't know enough about elephant reproduction to even manage ordinary IVF (in vitro fertilization) yet. The success rate of implanted cloned cells is so low that it would be impractical and unethical to try this with elephant surrogate mothers. We may be able to make progressively more mammoth-like elephant hybrids, but it will be a slow process.

How Did Birds Survive the Great Dinosaur Extinction?

Short answer: we don't know. Birds had already begun to evolve by the time of the extinction, but bird populations are very susceptible to storms and severe winters, let alone a major environmental disaster like a comet strike. There must be an explanation for the survival of birds (and turtles and crocs), but scientists are still looking for it.

Species like the European shag are vulnerable to increased storms due to climate change.

Were Dinosaurs Cold-Blooded Like Reptiles or Warm-Blooded Like Birds?

No one knows for sure. The old-school image of dinosaurs as cold-blooded, plodding reptiles went out of favor in the 1970s with new discoveries of agile, bird-like *Deinonychus*. Indeed, evidence from fossil bones suggests a rate of growth compatible with endothermic metabolism—that is, producing heat from within to maintain body temperature. Also, many dinosaurs lived in cold environments where getting enough heat from the surroundings might have been too difficult for cold-blooded animals to survive. Finally, some of the largest dinosaurs, such as *Brachiosaurus*, had such long necks that they would have needed endothermic metabolism to fuel their blood circulation. But some scientists think they had "mesothermic" metabolisms, somewhere between cold-blooded reptiles and warm-blooded birds.

How Did Pterosaurs Get Airborne?

With difficulty. The largest pterosaurs (which aren't classified as dinosaurs) were much bigger than even the largest flightless birds alive today. *Quetzlcoatlus*, for example, was the size of a giraffe, with a wingspan as wide as that of an F16 jet. Despite its incredible size, scientists have calculated that *Quetzlcoatlus* had sufficient bone strength and muscular power to allow a takeoff from a standing position, using its forelimbs to push off from the ground.

Quetzlcoatlus had the same wingspan as an F16 jet.

When Was the First Dinosaur Discovered?

Fossil bones exposed by rock falls and river erosion have been lying around in plain view for a lot longer than there have been humans. Chinese texts from 1100 BC mention dragon bones found in Sichuan province, which may have been dinosaur fossils. Greek legends of the Griffin, dating back to 675 BC, may have been based on *Protoceratops* skulls from Central Asia. But the first dinosaur to be described scientifically was a *Megalosaurus*, by British paleontologist William Buckland in 1824. The teeth and a few bones of an *Iguanodon* had been found two years previously by British geologist Mary Mantell, but the dinosaur itself wasn't described or named until 1825, after the *Megalosaurus*.

37 MPH (60KM/H)

The top speed of the fastest dinosaur, *Dromiceiomimus*—the same speed as that of a rhino, bison, and hyena

23

The number of letters in the longest dinosaur name— *Micropachycephalosaurus*

Time-travelling humans could come face-to-face with the predatory *Dimetrodon*: better hone those sprinting skills.

A scene from the 1975 film *One of Our Dinosaurs Is Missing.*

Could a Modern Human Survive on Pre-Dinosaur Earth?

It wouldn't be easy. The Permian period, just before the dinosaurs appeared, ran from about 299 to 251 million years ago. The drifting continental plates had clumped all the land together into one supercontinent called Pangaea. The huge size and limited coastline made the interior of Pangaea a hot desert, while the south was frozen under ice caps. The north was only slightly better, with a hot climate and huge seasonal variations from wet to dry. Flowering plants had only just started to appear and almost all the food crops we eat today hadn't evolved yet. We would be restricted to pine nuts and a few edible tubers. Most of our diet would probably consist of insects, but 90% of all insects at the start of the Permian were varieties of cockroach, so that's hardly an attractive prospect.

More importantly, we would still need to worry about being eaten. Just because the dinosaurs hadn't appeared yet, it doesn't mean there weren't large carnivores. *Dimetrodon* and other large crocodile-type animals were the top predators. Our intelligence and cooperation would help against these threats, but we would have to manage with primitive weaponry. And, the plant matter laid down in the Carboniferous period wouldn't turn into coal for another 100 million years yet, so we would have to make do with peat and pine wood for fuel, which would make it difficult to get a fire hot enough to smelt iron with.

Q & A

The ear is obviously visible in this image of a rhea.

What Did Dinosaurs Hear?

Through analyzing the inner ears of birds and extrapolating this upward to dinosaur sizes, researchers have been able to estimate hearing ranges. Large dinosaurs such as *T. rex* probably heard frequencies no higher than 3kHz. This would be enough to hear human speech fairly well, but is far below the top end of our hearing at 20kHz.

How Did Dinosaurs Mate?

No one really knows how *Brachiosaurus* mated.

Probably a bit like giraffes. We can't be sure because reproductive organs don't fossilize, and no fossils of dinosaurs caught in the act have ever been found. We don't even know for certain that dinosaurs had penises. We do know that the most primitive bird lineages have penises. An animal with a penis, and eggs with fertilized shells, suggests internal fertilization. The problem is how a female *Brachiosaurus* managed to avoid being crushed beneath the weight of an 18-ton (16-tonne) male. It would certainly have been a precarious business, but not (ahem) insurmountable. The actual moment of copulation was probably very brief, to minimize the mechanical stresses.

Why Did *T. rex* Have Tiny Arms?

Poor *T. rex*. Its body looks so strong, but its arms look so weak. While its arms were incredibly short, they were also very muscular. So they must have been doing something. Otherwise, evolution would have gotten rid of them, the same way that hind limbs on whales disappeared when they were no longer needed. The arms of a *T. rex* might have been used to grip prey or push up with if the beast fell over.

And you thought peeling sunburn was bad . . .

Did Dinosaurs Shed Their Skins, Like Most Modern Reptiles?

All vertebrates shed their skin, along with virtually all animals that actually have a skin. The difference is that most of them don't shed it all in one piece. But neither do all reptiles. Molting a complete skin in one go seems to be restricted to snakes, legless lizards (like the slowworm), and some soft-shelled turtles. Presumably, this is because they have flexible, streamlined body shapes that make it easy to wriggle out of their old skins. Most lizards shed their skins in small patches. Crocs and other large reptiles have much thicker scales for protection, and shedding the entire skin would leave them too vulnerable while the new one hardened. Instead they shed individual scales—a model copied by mammals and birds. It seems overwhelmingly likely that dinosaurs, from whom birds have evolved, would have also shed their skin one piece at a time or in small patches.

IN NUMBERS

22¾
The length of a day during the Triassic period—shorter than today because Earth was rotating faster

80
The lifespan of a sauropod—much longer than the 30 years most other dinosaurs lasted

Could a Dinosaur Survive in Today's Climate Conditions?

No one knows for sure. Atmospheric conditions were certainly different from today. Recent studies suggest oxygen levels in the Mesozoic were low and carbon dioxide levels high, so they might have struggled to survive from that perspective. But, many dinosaurs would have been fine in current subtropical and temperate climates—and could even have flourished (see page 96). The one thing they couldn't deal with is recently evolved microbes.

Q & A

How Do Dinosaurs Get Their Names?

Most dinosaurs are named after a prominent physical feature or behavior, using Greek or Latin words to make the name international. So *Triceratops* means "three-horned head," while *Stegosaurus* means "covered lizard" or "roof lizard" because of the plates that run along its spine. Others are named after the place in which their fossils were first discovered (*Argentinosaurus*, *Denversaurus*) or in memory of their discoverer, such as *Lambeosaurus*, named after Lawrence Lambe. Like the scientific names of all living animals, dinosaur names must be ratified by the International Commission on Zoological Nomenclature to keep names consistent and avoid duplication.

Triceratops means "three-horned head."

Were Dinosaur Eggs the Same Shape As Bird Eggs?

The basic constraint on the shape of an egg is that it must fit through the pelvic canal. The shell is still somewhat pliable when it is laid, and the squeezing from the pelvic muscles tends to form an ovoid (the word comes from the Latin for "egg") with a tapering rear end. Birds with large clutch sizes tend to have more rounded eggs because these pack better within the oviduct—the passage leading from the ovaries to the vagina—and stay warmer in the nest. Birds that nest on cliff ledges, like the guillemot, have pointier eggs that roll in a tight circle. Dinosaurs nested on the ground, so their eggs were more symmetrical. But they were also more elongated because this allows for a larger embryo, while still allowing the egg to fit through a narrow opening.

DINOSAUR BODY SHAPES

THE KEY CHARACTERISTICS OF EACH GROUP REFLECTS THEIR HABITATS AND LIFESTYLES

SAUROPODS
Quadrupedal, herbivorous dinosaurs. The group includes some of the largest land animals ever to exist.

CERATOPIANS
Medium-sized dinosaurs with varying sized solid frills and beaks forming an overbite. Ceratopsidae also had horns.

EUORNITHOPODS
Bipedal "bird-footed" dinosaurs with horned beaks, muscular hind legs, and shorter front legs.

Getting dino DNA from a mosquito trapped in amber would be virtually impossible.

A fossilized dinosaur nest, with a hen's egg for size comparison.

Could Dinosaur DNA Come from a Mosquito in Amber?

It's next to impossible. First, a mosquito that has bitten a dinosaur must get itself stuck in resin before it has had a chance to digest its blood meal completely. Next, it must quickly dry out within the resin to the point where processes involving enzymes (proteins that act as catalysts in biochemical reactions) have stopped. This is unlikely—tree resin is viscous and does not mix with water. Long after the mosquito had suffocated in the resin, the contents of its stomach would continue to break down. Any remaining DNA must then survive the heat, pressure, and passage of millions of years as the resin turns to amber. We would then need to extract this DNA, separate each fragment according to the animal it came from, and insert them into the germ line of a sufficiently similar reptile or bird. Then we would have to stand back and hope the resultant creature grows to maturity and retains the physical characteristics of the original dinosaur.

LARGE THEROPODS
Monstrous, "bird-footed" killers with two powerful hind legs, tiny front arms, and hollow bones.

SMALL THEROPODS
Smaller, more agile versions, often feathered and with more diverse features among species.

ANKYLOSAURIDS
Stocky bodies covered in tough bony plates and lumps. Some had clubbed tails and horns.

ORNITHOMIMOSAURS
Tiny heads containing toothless beaks, long necks, and long legs ending in three-toed feet.

VELOCIRAPTOR

DESPITE ITS SMALL SIZE, THIS FEISTY CARNIVORE WAS A FORCE TO BE RECKONED WITH

LONG, RIGID TAIL FOR BALANCE

The small, swift, and nimble dinosaur was a lethal predator. It had a long snout and slender jaws, housing 28 dagger-like teeth. An enormous, curved talon on each foot was used to pin down struggling prey—anything from insects to other dinosaurs. When not in use, the talon was raised up off the ground. *Velociraptor*'s body was fully covered in a bird-like plumage.

A GIANT TALON ON EACH FOOT WAS USED TO TRAP PREY.

APPROXIMATE SIZE COMPARISON

THE SMALL BODY WAS THE SIZE OF A LARGE TURKEY.

UP TO 28 SERRATED, RAZOR-SHARP TEETH

FEATHERS COVERED THE WHOLE BODY BUT WERE USELESS FOR FLIGHT.

DID YOU KNOW?

Velociraptor was 12 times shorter than *T. rex* but could run faster at a maximum speed of 25 miles per hour (40km/h).

FACT FILE

MEANING OF NAME: Quick plunderer

PRONOUNCED: Vel-oss-ee-rap-tor

SIZE: 6 feet (1.8m) long, 1.6 feet (0.5m) tall, 15–33 pounds (7–15kg)

DIET: Amphibians, insects, reptiles, mammals, pterosaurs, and other dinosaurs (like *Protoceratops*)

WHEN IT LIVED: Late Cretaceous (84–80 million years ago)

DISCOVERED BY: Henry F. Osborn in 1924

Velociraptor

THE DAY THE DINOSAURS DIED

Scientists have drilled into the heart of the Chicxulub crater—the landing site of the meteorite that killed the dinosaurs. Here are their latest discoveries.

Text by Henry Nicholls, a science writer and author.
He tweets from @WayOfThePanda.

THE STORY OF THE CRATER

In the late 1970s, the Mexican oil company Pemex was scouring the Gulf of Mexico for possible sites to drill. A ring of mountains on the ocean floor with a diameter of around 44 miles (70km) sparked the interest of Pemex geologist Glen Penfield.

Further scrutiny of the Yucatán Peninsula revealed another concentric ring, strongly suggesting some kind of catastrophic impact, with its center lying close to what is now the small coastal town of Chicxulub.

When a young University of Arizona graduate named Alan Hildebrand got in touch with Penfield, they teamed up and tracked down cores from three deep exploration wells that Pemex had drilled within the region (C1, S1 and Y6 in the gravity map right). In these rocks, they found evidence of a cataclysmic event at precisely the moment the dinosaurs vanished, at the end of the Cretaceous Period.

Now scientists have drilled deeper into the crater than ever before (Chicx-03A, right).

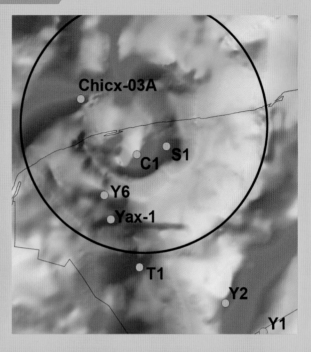

The meteorite left a crater 124 miles (200km) across when it smashed into the planet. Today, this geological scar lies buried beneath the Yucatán Peninsula.

Core 40: To the untrained eye, this 10-foot (3-m) section of rock winched up from a borehole beneath the Gulf of Mexico might not look like much. But for Professor Sean Gulick, a geologist at the University of Texas, it's a sample that holds secrets about one of the most catastrophic events in the history of planet Earth.

For Gulick, the core will tell him the story of the day the Earth shook. Sixty-six million years ago, a 46 foot (14km)-wide meteorite slammed into our planet. Wildfires raged, earthquakes rumbled, and a dusty curtain fell upon the Earth. It was the beginning of the end for around 75% of the planet's species, including all nonavian dinosaurs.

Travelling at 12 miles per second (20km/second) when it entered Earth's atmosphere, the meteorite left a crater 124 miles (200km) across when it smashed into the planet. Today, this geological scar lies buried beneath the Yucatán Peninsula in southeastern Mexico—and now, for the first time, we've drilled into its heart.

Throughout April and May 2016, Gulick was stationed on a drilling rig just off the Yucatán Peninsula. He was the co-chief scientist on Expedition 364, the joint project by the International Continental Drilling Program and International Ocean Discovery Program to drill down into the Chicxulub impact crater. On this boat-cum-drilling platform, 19 miles (30km) off the Mexican coast, his team worked day and night to bore down to over 0.81 miles (1.3km) beneath the seabed to extract precious cores of rock.

Since these cores were cracked open in autumn of 2016, geologists, physicists, chemists, and biologists have been trying to piece together what happened in the minutes, hours, days, and years after touchdown. Analysis is still ongoing. What they find could help us to understand why this single rock had such lethal and far-reaching consequences across the entire planet. It could also explain how life was able to recover following the impact.

Expedition 364 set up a scientific platform in the ocean and spent April and May 2016 drilling into the seabed to extract core samples from the Chicxulub impact crater.

Drilling to Doomsday

Core 40 is of interest because this section may help explain how one asteroid (or comet) could have had such global consequences. Up to this point, the team had pulled out 39 cores of limestone all the way from 1,640 miles (500m) to 2,034 miles (620m) below the seabed. "Then suddenly we hit a layer with fragments in it," says Gulick.

They had found the top of a thick blanket of "breccia," a jumbled layer of the shattered, melted, and traumatized debris that settled in the minutes or hours after impact. "I didn't expect it to be this nice, sharp transition from limestone, boom, right into angular material with melt in it," says Gulick.

Of particular interest are the microfossils that sit just above this breccia, which should paint a vivid picture of the local conditions in the immediate aftermath. One of those given the responsibility of studying these fossils was Chris Lowery, a post-doctoral studies student in paleontology at the University of Texas.

A foraminifera fossil. These tiny creatures proliferated and diversified rapidly after the Chicxulub impact.

CROSS SECTION OF THE CRATER

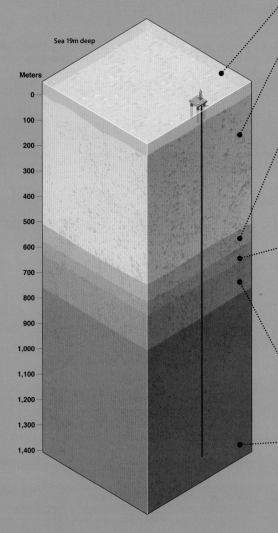

Sea 19m deep

Meters

0
100
200
300
400
500
600
700
800
900
1,000
1,100
1,200
1,300
1,400

0 feet (0m)
Seabed.

1,650 feet (503m)
Coring begins. As the focus of the expedition is on the impact crater, the scientists race through the first 1,640 feet (500m) of limestone before beginning to pull up cores of rock, 10 feet (3m) at a time.

1,805 feet (550m)
Algal blooms. Around 55 million years ago, some 10 million years after the asteroid impact, the Earth was around 5°C warmer than at present. Scientists are hoping to recover black shales, the geological remnants of carbon-rich algal blooms predicted to have thrived in the warmer conditions.

1,805–2,034 feet (550–620m)
Approaching ground zero. As the drill reaches the top of the impact layer, the ecology is expected to thin out to just a few rather simple species. By studying the chemical makeup of the very first foraminifera to colonize the site after the impact, it should be possible to infer the local conditions at the time.

2,034–2,428 feet (620–740m)
The impact layer is a chaotic mix of fragmented rocks and melt that settled in the minutes and hours after the asteroid hit. It could contain microorganisms that took up residence in the aftermath to capitalize on the rich chemistry.

2,428–4,380 feet (740–1,335m)
The peak ring. By paying special attention to the age and sequence of rocks in the peak ring, geologists hope to solve the mystery of how these structures form. Satellite data indicates that the rock in the peak ring is not as dense as it might be. Are there cracks and fissures, and what kind of microbes might live in these voids?

A PLANET IN SHOCK

EARTH IN THE HOURS, YEARS, AND MILLENNIA AFTER THE IMPACT

HOURS
Huge earthquakes, mega-tsunamis up to 984 feet (300m) high, winds of over 620 miles per hour (1,000km/h), and rampant wildfires result in instant annihilation for many species.

WEEKS
Dust from the impact and soot from wildfires block out sunlight for many years. Plants that survived the impact soon struggle. Food webs start to unravel.

YEARS
Prior to the impact, nonavian dinosaurs are already in decline, but the impact seals their fate. If any species survive the impact, it's not for long. Over 90% of all mammal species also go extinct. The largest mammals are hardest hit; the survivors are all smaller than a cat. On land, forests and flowering plants struggle with the low light levels, resulting in a preponderance of species like ferns, algae, and moss.

Artist's impression of the Chicxulub crater shortly after impact. The inner "peak ring" is where scientists are focusing their efforts today.

"I've lain awake at night sometimes, wondering what we've got in core 40," he enthuses. "This is the kind of thing I got into science to do. It's so cool to be part of something like this."

Lowery's expertise is in foraminifera, single-celled creatures that often boast beautifully complex internal shells or "tests." By studying the chemical makeup of these fossilized structures, he's attempting to reconstruct the temperature, salinity, and local productivity of the water that filled the crater, giving an insight into the kind of environment that survivors of the asteroid would have faced.

Based on work elsewhere, we know that the asteroid impact led to the extinction of more than 90% of all floating, plankton-like foraminifera. The species that survived were typically small and generalist, but within a mere 100,000 years they had diversified into dozens of different species. "It's exciting to see here at ground zero what the properties of the ocean were that might have driven that evolution," says Lowery.

Meanwhile, analysis of the carbon isotopes in the rock core will help us to understand how the carbon cycle was affected by the impact. This in turn will tell us more about the response of the world's plants to the event—and the dinosaurs that depended on them. Similar analysis has been carried out elsewhere, but the Chicxulub cores contain large amounts of material, so it should be possible to build up a more accurate, high-resolution picture of the events that led to a mass extinction.

300,000 YEARS
Because mammals from several different groups survived, mammal diversity recovers quite quickly, soon doubling the number of species before the extinction.

1 MILLION YEARS
Deciduous trees, reliant on wind pollination, begin to return. Evergreens, which rely on insects and animals for reproduction, take longer to bounce back.

3 MILLION YEARS
In the oceans, there is a rapid flourishing of the plankton-like floating foraminifera. This contributes to the recovery of most marine systems.

10 MILLION YEARS
The surviving reptiles are quick to diversify, with the appearance of iguanas, monitor lizards, and boas. Many insect lineages survive the impact. After the event, ants and termites increase in their diversity. Butterflies also spread their wings.

15 MILLION YEARS
In a few million years the ancestors of most modern birds undergo a rapid evolution into the multitude of lineages and thousands of species we see today.

A clump of breccia recovered from the impact crater.

USA

Gulf of Mexico

Drill Site

Chicxulub crater

The drill site
lies 19 miles (30km)
off the coast of Mexico.

N

200km

Life Down Below?

There might even be signs of actual life in the rubble-like breccia and beneath—microorganisms that have been living and evolving deep underground for many millions of years.

"Most of life on Earth is underground," says Charles Cockell, an astrobiologist at the University of Edinburgh. "Something like a massive asteroid impact that killed off the dinosaurs would also have dramatically disrupted the deep biosphere, particularly at the place of impact," he says. "But it may not necessarily have been all bad."

A decade ago, Cockell was part of a similar project on the Chesapeake Bay in Virginia on the East Coast of the United States, the site of a smaller and, at 35 million years old, more recent impact. This event appears to have fractured the underlying rock,

improving the flow of water and creating a habitat that would have been particularly suited to microbial life. "We found there was an increase in the numbers of microbes in impact-fractured rocks."

A similar thing may have occurred at Chicxulub, with the molten rock created by the impact setting up a "hydrothermal system" also suitable for life.

"The breccia is almost like chicken soup for microbes," says Cockell. "It's got everything in it that's leaching out and providing food for microbes."

Further down, in the underlying granite, the trauma caused by the impact may have created new opportunities for microorganisms. "At the immediate point of impact, everything would have been sterilized, so it was certainly bad for them in the

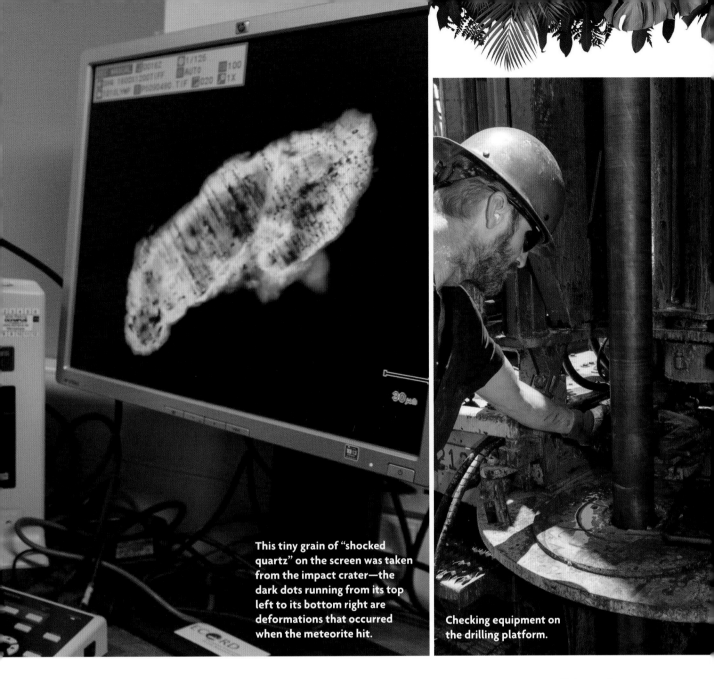

This tiny grain of "shocked quartz" on the screen was taken from the impact crater—the dark dots running from its top left to its bottom right are deformations that occurred when the meteorite hit.

Checking equipment on the drilling platform.

same moment it was bad for the dinosaurs," he says. "But in the longer term, it will have improved conditions for life."

Through analysis of the rock cores, the researchers are homing in on the date at which the hydrothermal system cooled down enough to allow the microbes to exploit the chemicals dissolved in the hot fluids for fuel. Earth's magnetic field flips direction every few hundred thousand years. At the time of the Chicxulub extinction event, the magnetic field had the reverse polarity to that of today. However, samples of rock with both "normal" and reverse polarity were found within the core. As the polarity is "recorded" by molten rock as it cools, this suggests that the rock at ground zero remained fluid until the field flipped around 300,000 years after impact.

If the researchers' model is correct, then all this implies that any impact crater could have been a suitable spot for the origin of life on Earth more than 3.5 billion years ago. Though the conditions at the time of the Chicxulub impact were "radically different" from those on the early Earth, says Cockell, the subsurface microbial ecosystem under the Gulf of Mexico could hint at some of the biochemical challenges that the first life forms would have faced. In time, the rock cores will likely reveal more secrets about how microbes were able to adapt to the conditions in the breccia.

Dust from the impact cloaked the planet in darkness, leading to the widespread collapse of food webs.

Crater Conundrums

In the days before drilling began, there was a lot of nervous excitement among the scientists involved. "I was super stressed before I got on the platform," admits Joanna Morgan, a geophysicist at Imperial College London and co-chief scientist of the expedition along with Gulick. But as soon as the "super-gorgeous" cores began to come out of the ground, the stress just vanished, adds Morgan.

That said, not everything went smoothly. Early on in the project, a 656-foot (200-m) piece of piping fell to the bottom of the hole, putting a complete stop to drilling. "The whole thing was a good week of nail-biting before we actually got the first 50-million-year-old core just below that point," says Gulick.

But apart from this glitch, everything went pretty much to plan, with cores being pulled up to the surface 24 hours a day, seven

I was super stressed before I got on the platform. When the super-gorgeous cores began to come out of the ground, the stress vanished.

days a week. "Sometimes we would succeed in coring 98 feet [30m] a day," says Gulick. When the money ran out and it was time to withdraw the drill at the end of May, the hole stretched for 4,380 feet (1,335m) below the seabed.

The deeper cores will be of special interest to geologists like Gulick and Morgan, as they should help account for the formation of the so-called "peak ring," a circular mountain range that lies within the

WHAT REALLY KILLED THE DINOSAURS?

In 1980, Nobel Prize-winning physicist Luis Alvarez and his team discovered a thin layer of iridium blanketing Earth at precisely the moment when the dinosaurs disappeared from the fossil record. As iridium is one of the rarest elements in Earth's crust, but is found in asteroids in far higher concentrations, the scientists imagined vast quantities of dust (including extraterrestrial iridium) propelled high into the stratosphere and distributed worldwide.

"The resulting darkness would suppress photosynthesis," they wrote in *Science*, which would have led to the rapid collapse of food webs and the demise of the dinosaurs. A decade later, in 1990, geologists identified Chicxulub in the Gulf of Mexico as the most likely site of this impact.

Few scientists now dispute the terminal consequences of the Chicxulub event for many species, but there is also evidence to suggest that other factors could have been part of the dinosaurs' demise. The Deccan Traps, in what is now central India, are one of the largest volcanic features on Earth. There is some uncertainty over exactly when they formed—it could have been just before the asteroid impact or as a result of the aftershock—but the volcanic gases released would have had a chilling effect on the climate. It seems likely that the Chicxulub impact would also have triggered a wave of secondary events, like earthquakes, mega-tsunamis, wildfires, volcanism, and acid rain, that could all have helped push Earth's reptilian rulers over the edge.

crater, roughly midway between the center and the rim. According to Gulick, we can also see structures like this on the Moon, Mercury, and Mars, "but we haven't gone and gotten those rocks," he says.

At Chicxulub, on the other hand, the scientists have drilled right into the peak ring. "It's the only well-preserved large impact on Earth, so we can test the fundamental ways that impact cratering affects a planet," he explains.

The prevailing model to explain this mountainous ring is that following the initial impact there was some kind of rebound of fractured rocks at the center of the crater, which rippled outwards before eventually coming to a stop. To picture this, think of what happens when you throw a stone into a pond.

Superficially, the rock in these deeper cores looks just like normal granite, says Morgan. "Except when you look closely, it's very highly fractured," she says. "It has a very strange set of

> It's the only well-preserved large impact on Earth, so we can test the fundamental ways that impact cratering affects a planet.

physical properties. I think it's going to explain to us how rocks that are really hard are weakened enough to be able to move many, many miles [km] during this impact event."

The cores, and all the valuable clues they contain, have been analyzed in detail—and some of the results are in. Early results suggest that the hydrothermal system generated by the impact was not strong enough to prevent life re-colonizing the seafloor relatively quickly.

The Day the Dinosaurs Died

BRACHIOSAURUS

DESPITE THE NECK OF THIS MIGHTY, LATE JURASSIC HERBIVORE BEING ITS DEFINING FEATURE, *BRACHIOSAURUS* MEANS "ARM LIZARD."

Paleontologists know that *Brachiosaurus* had an incredibly long neck, formed of 13 long, air-filled neck bones. The neck was flexible and mostly held erect. Due to its colossal size and herbivorous diet, it had to eat around 880 pounds (400kg) every day. Once thought to have made its home in water because of the high position of its bony nostril openings, it is now understood that it had nostrils close to the front of its snout and, hence, lived on land. It probably roamed in herds in dry, park-like environments.

LONG LEGS THAT ARE LONGER AND MORE SLENDER THAN THOSE OF MOST OTHER SAUROPODS

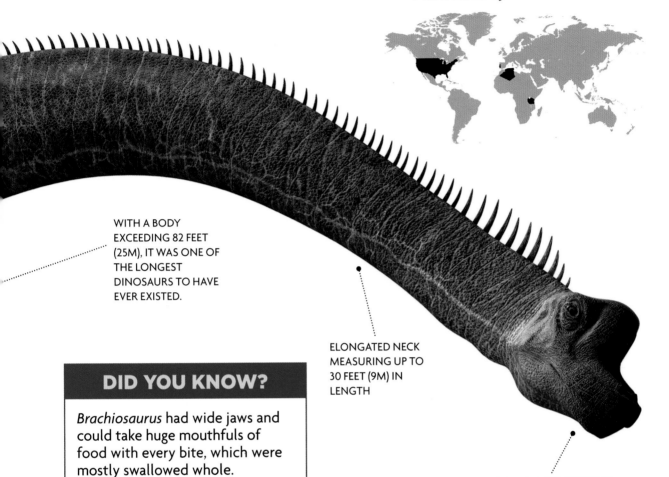

WITH A BODY EXCEEDING 82 FEET (25M), IT WAS ONE OF THE LONGEST DINOSAURS TO HAVE EVER EXISTED.

ELONGATED NECK MEASURING UP TO 30 FEET (9M) IN LENGTH

DID YOU KNOW?

Brachiosaurus had wide jaws and could take huge mouthfuls of food with every bite, which were mostly swallowed whole.

SPOON-SHAPED TEETH TO EFFICIENTLY STRIP LEAVES FROM STEMS AND BRANCHES

FACT FILE

MEANING OF NAME: Arm lizard

PRONOUNCED: Brak-ee-oh-sore-us

SIZE: 98 feet (30m) long, 23 feet (7m) tall at shoulder, 12,000 pounds (5,500kg)

DIET: Tall vegetation

WHEN IT LIVED: Late Jurassic (155–140 million years ago)

DISCOVERED BY: Elmer Riggs in 1900

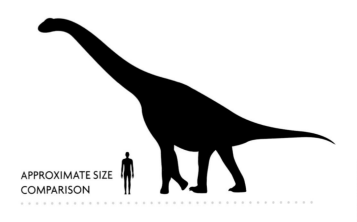

APPROXIMATE SIZE COMPARISON

Brachiosaurus

WHAT IF THE DINOSAURS HAD SURVIVED?

If the dinosaurs hadn't been wiped out in a mass extinction 66 million years ago, the world would look very different today. We might still have evolved alongside them.

Text by John Pickrell, science journalist and author of *Flying Dinosaurs*
Illustrations by James Gilleard

An estimated 17 billion tons (15 billion tonnes) of soot spread through the atmosphere, creating one long night that lasted several years, making photosynthesis all but impossible and heralding an endless winter that saw average temperatures fall. This was the fate awaiting those few wretched creatures that survived the initial impact of a 9 mile (14km)-wide asteroid 66 million years ago—and the earthquakes, tsunamis, wildfires, and volcanic eruptions that swiftly followed in its wake.

Around three-quarters of all species went extinct, and no animal bigger than a Labrador retriever survived, but things could have been very different according to researchers at the University of Texas. They reported findings that if the asteroid struck Earth just a few minutes earlier, it would have hit deep ocean, rather than the shallow sea of the Yucatan Peninsula in present-day Mexico, and the outcome could have been quite different.

Had that been the case, then the damage would have been more localized. Some of the dinosaurs far from the impact site might have survived, and the world would be a very different place today. In our own history, only the feathered theropod dinosaurs we know as birds made it through this calamity, but how would things have turned out if their larger relatives had joined them? Would dinosaurs still be alive today and could mammals such as humans have evolved? What would our world look like if we shared it with the descendants of animals like *T. rex* and *Triceratops*?

"I'm sure a fairly nice diversity of nonavian dinosaurs would still be here," says Dr. Stephen Brusatte, a paleontologist at the University of Edinburgh. "If there was no sudden, catastrophic shock of the asteroid, I really don't see anything that's happened since—whether it was the spread of grasslands; changing ocean currents; the separation of Antarctica from South America, which caused a cold snap; or the more recent Ice Ages—that would have knocked off the dinosaurs."

Over the years many have tried to imagine what kind of creatures dinosaurs might have evolved into if they had survived. The most famous attempt is a 1988 book called *The New Dinosaurs: An Alternative Evolution*, by Scottish geologist and author Dougal Dixon. For this magnificent work of speculative zoology, Dixon conjured up creatures such as the "cutlasstooth"—a pack-hunting, saber-toothed predator from South America; the "cribrum"—a flamingo-like, filter-feeding theropod from Australia; and the "gourmand"—a relative of *T. rex* that lost its front limbs entirely and developed a distensible jaw to allow it to rapidly swallow prey whole, much like a snake.

Perhaps this last idea isn't entirely wide of the mark. Dr. Tom Holtz, an expert on theropod dinosaurs at the University of Maryland in the United States, says that both tyrannosaurs and abelisaurs, the types of big meat-eaters present in the Late Cretaceous, are notable for

their very small forelimbs. "Given that arms were noncritical for hunting, it's possible that a Cenozoic tyrannosaur could have been armless," says Holtz.

The beginning of the Cenozoic Era (which spans the period from 66 million years ago until the present day) might essentially have been an ecological extension of the Late Cretaceous. Creatures such as titanosaur sauropods, duck-billed hadrosaurs, horned ceratopsians, and predators such as tyrannosaurs and abelisaurs would have remained common.

But as we head further from the Cretaceous toward the present, there would likely have been significant changes, says Dr. Andy Farke at the Raymond M. Alf Museum of Paleontology in Claremont, California. "If dinosaurs were still around today, they'd be pretty different to what we think of at the end of the age of the dinosaurs—things like *T. rex* and *Triceratops*," he argues. "You might still recognize them as a dinosaur, but who knows what kind of body shapes and body plans might have come up in the past 66 million years."

Many of the kinds of mammals we're familiar with might not have had the opportunity to evolve. "You can't underestimate the importance of that extinction 66 million years ago in really hitting the reset button for mammals and clearing the playing field," adds Farke.

HAD DINOSAURS SURVIVED AND EVOLVED, ALL KINDS OF NEW BODY FORMS MIGHT HAVE DEVELOPED.

❶ Dino-monkeys

Once flowering plants appeared in the Cretaceous, there was no stopping them. In the Cenozoic, fruit became abundant across the world, and tree-dwelling, primate-like feathered dinosaurs may have evolved to take advantage of the sugary goodness.

❷ Burrow dwellers

Curiously, few known dinosaurs appear to have used burrows. Perhaps given more time, rodent- or mole-like species may have evolved to exploit the subterranean environment.

❸ Woolly wonders

Many theropod dinosaurs had feathers, and we know some lived at Arctic latitudes. Perhaps both carnivores and herbivores would have developed thick, shaggy pelts during the Ice Ages, something akin to musk ox, woolly rhinos, or mammoths.

❹ Grassland grazers

As the world cooled 34 million years ago at the end of the Eocene, forests retreated and grasslands spread globally. Slender, speedy dinosaurs with teeth specialized for cropping grasses would likely have evolved to devour this new resource.

❺ Whale-o-saurs

Unlike their relatives—the mosasaurs, ichthyosaurs, and plesiosaurs—few dinosaurs exploited marine environments. Perhaps creatures similar to Spinosaurus could eventually have become dinosaurian filter-feeding equivalents of baleen whales.

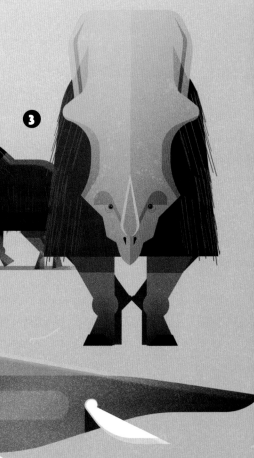

Dinosaurs: The Myth-Busting Guide to Prehistoric Beasts

Some dinosaurs might have followed mammals, such as manatees, back into the oceans.

Tree Huggers

Already in the Cretaceous there were numerous fluffy, feathered theropods scampering in the trees. Assuming flowering plants continued to spread and thrive as they did in our history, then could primate-like dinosaurs have specialized to take advantage of the fruit they produced? Professor Matthew Bonnan, a paleobiologist at Stockton University in New Jersey, argues that primates evolved large, forward-facing eyes with color vision to forage for fruit.

"Is there a connection between being frugivorous and having a larger brain? We don't know, but one could imagine arboreal dinosaurs that formed a coevolutionary relationship with flowering plants by eating their fruits and dispersing the seeds," he says. "Whether these fruit-eating dinosaurs would have evolved complex social groups like primates is pure speculation."

Other ecological spaces little explored by dinosaurs were aquatic environments.

"In mammals we've seen a return to the sea, in several different iterations," says Farke. "We've had things like whales and manatees that have gone back into the oceans, and things like otters that

spend a lot of time in the water. It's cool to think about what dinosaurs could have looked like if they'd gone in a cetacean direction."

But if their giant marine reptile relatives—the mosasaurs and plesiosaurs—had survived, then dinosaurs might have found it hard to get a foothold.

There could also have been other consequences of dinosaurs and their reptilian relatives, such as the flying pterosaurs, not dying out at the end of the Cretaceous. Although birds coexisted with dinosaurs for a long time in the Cretaceous, their diversity was low compared to today. "Modern bird groups underwent an explosive radiation after the mass extinction, maybe because pterosaurs went extinct and opened up new niches," says Dr. Victoria Arbour, a paleontologist at the Royal Ontario Museum in Toronto. "Without the mass extinction, maybe birds wouldn't be as diverse and successful as they are today—and maybe we wouldn't have things like songbirds, parrots, hawks, or hummingbirds at all."

Most experts seem to agree that the largest land mammals— elephants, mammoths, giant relatives of rhinos and sloths, perhaps even horses and giraffes—probably couldn't have evolved if large

**Mammoths might not have evolved
if dinosaurs had survived.**

dinosaurs had remained to occupy the niches they came to fill.

But perhaps smaller mammals such as rodents, bats, and primates would have been just as successful. If that had been the case, then some of those primates could have climbed down from the trees onto the grasslands and savannahs that eventually replaced the thick forests of the Cretaceous, and evolved into hominids, as our ancestors did.

"If we speculate that humans had evolved alongside dinosaurs, then they probably would have been able to coexist," says Farke. "Humans already evolved in ecosystems that had large land animals and predators. We probably would have done ok."

"Unarmed, solitary humans are still easy targets for large predators today—like bears and lions," agrees Arbour. "But overall, humans are pretty good at surviving alongside large, dangerous animals."

> Overall, humans are pretty
> good at surviving alongside
> large, dangerous animals.

Cenozoic Extinction

Dinosaurs might not have been so lucky, though, as humans seem to have a special skill for killing off large animals. Perhaps the biggest dinosaurs would have gone the way of the mammoth and the dodo. "Humans are really good at extinguishing megafauna—through hunting, climate change, or habitat destruction," Arbour says. "Dinosaurs in the twenty-first century, just like modern animals, would probably have reduced populations and face the threat of extinction."

Big dinosaurs would perhaps only persist in protected reserves, such as national parks and wildlife refuges—modern-day equivalents of *Jurassic Park*. Smaller dinosaurs "that infringed on crops or livestock would probably be hunted as 'nuisance' animals" as wolves and dingoes are today, adds Arbour. "It would be really hard for large sauropods to survive alongside us. They're so big and would require so much food, that I doubt we could set aside enough wild spaces for them to thrive."

City Dwellers

The kinds of dinosaurs that might do well are those that could learn to live and thrive alongside people. In our world today, the

JURASSIC EXPLOITATION

WE HAVE DOMESTICATED SPECIES SUCH AS HORSES, COWS, CHICKENS, AND SHEEP. HAD DINOSAURS SURVIVED, MIGHT WE HAVE USED THEM FOR LABOR AND FOOD— OR HUNTED THEM AS TROPHIES?

In the 1960s cartoon series *The Flintstones*, Fred works as a "bronto crane operator" riding a sauropod, which does the heavy lifting in a quarry. It seems unlikely, in reality, that we would ever have been able to domesticate and persuade dinosaurs weighing many tens of tons (tonnes) to do work for us in agrarian societies—as humans did with oxen and horses.

"Given the brainpower of some of these dinosaurs, I can't imagine that a lot of them would be in the realm of things that would domesticate easily," says Dr. Andy Farke.

But there may have been other ways humanity could have exploited dinosaurs.

"Animals that have been domesticated by humans are often those that have group social structures like wolves, caribou, and cattle," says Dr. Victoria Arbour. "For dinosaurs, herding species like ceratopsians and hadrosaurs might have been good candidates for cattle analogs. There's less evidence for social behavior in small carnivores, but perhaps some little predatory, feathery theropods might have filled the spots in our homes reserved for dogs and cats today."

Had we exploited some of these larger herbivores to toil in our fields, surely, we would have hunted and farmed some for meat too? Which begs the question: what would dinosaur meat have

tasted like? Of course, if you eat chicken or turkey today, then you are already eating theropod dinosaur, but the flesh of these sedentary, domesticated creatures is a poor analogy for *T. rex* meat—a much better one might be emu or ostrich, which are fast-runners packed with lean muscle.

"Just as with modern farming, there'd probably be the whole thing with wanting to get organically raised or free-range dinosaur meat—or corn-fed *Triceratops*," quips Farke. Ostriches are farmed today, so some of the fast-running, ostrich-like ornithomimid dinosaurs, such as *Gallimimus* (famous from the stampede scene in *Jurassic Park*), could have populated ranches in the same way. Battery farms of egg-laying dinosaurs could also have been a possibility. "The glorious thing about dinosaurs is that they grew very quickly," says Farke.

Given that today there are certain types of wealthy gun-lovers who will pay significant sums to shoot lions, rhinos, and giraffes on private game reserves—had dinosaurs survived to the present, then they would surely be the ultimate in big game. Horned dinosaurs, duckbills, and even carnivores of the ilk of *T. rex* could have been targets, argues Arbour: "Big ceratopsians, hadrosaurs and theropods would probably be highly sought after for trophy hunting."

MAN'S BEST FRIEND?

THE MOST MASSIVE AND FEROCIOUS DINOSAURS WOULD HAVE BEEN TERRIBLE PETS FOR OBVIOUS REASONS, BUT USE YOUR IMAGINATION TO SEE HOW SMALLER DINOS MIGHT HAVE MADE BETTER COMPANIONS.

Microraptor

Dark and glossy iridescent plumage, with large flight feathers on its hind and forelimbs, making for a beautiful pet. Likes to preen, nap, and observe everything with its hawklike, watchful eyes.

SIZE: One of the very smallest dinosaurs at less than 2 pounds (1kg) in weight and about 32 inches (80cm) in length

PROS: Four wings of awesomeness; intelligent and responds well to commands

CONS: Can attempt to disembowel the cat with its sickle-shaped second claw; requires falconry hood during initial training

Sinosauropteryx

The first known feathered dinosaur, found in 1996. This relative of *Compsognathus* has lovely, fluffy ginger plumage and enjoys scratches and strokes. Likes to chase toys in lieu of fast-moving prey.

SIZE: 3 feet (1m) in length including the long tail but very dainty, weighing just 1 pound (0.5kg)

PROS: Loves to snuggle; attractive ginger-and-white tail stripes

CONS: Can be neurotic and restless; requires frequent exercise

majority of animal biomass is made up of species that we farm or have domesticated, or those that live around our cities and developments—and so it would also have been in a reality where humans and dinosaurs coexisted. There might have been dinosaur equivalents of seagulls, pigeons, rats, raccoons, and foxes—all very well adapted to take advantage of the resources available in urban environments.

"Small, scrappy dinosaurs might have been able to eke out a living on the margins of housing developments," suggests Farke. You can imagine slender little beaked hypsilophodont herbivores nibbling at the roses and hydrangeas in your garden.

"Animals that do well in urban environments today tend to be those that are good at eating whatever we're throwing away, and making use of the structures we build," agrees Arbour. "Small omnivorous or predatory theropods, like the descendants of oviraptorosaurs and troodontids, would perhaps have been lurking around garbage cans."

Obviously, we might have domesticated dinosaurs to exploit for meat and eggs or agricultural labor, and we would very likely have taken them into our homes as pets—the feathery or scaly equivalents of dogs and cats.

Perhaps, though, the idea that humans could have evolved in a world filled with dinosaurs is simply too far-fetched. "I have no doubt that we would not be here," says

Dinosaurs that could live alongside people would have been the ones that thrived.

Psittacosaurus

This parrot-beaked herbivore was a compact, primitive ceratopsian and would have made a good pet. Lives in herds in the wild, so highly sociable and has a fairly gentle temperament.

SIZE: Up to 7 feet (2m) in length and 44 pounds (20kg) in weight

PROS: Fluffy tail bristles; cute facial horns; helps to keep the lawn tidy by mowing grass with beak

CONS: Tendency to gnaw the furniture

Yi Qi

This teeny, pigeon-sized tree-dweller is the only dinosaur known to have adopted a bat method of flight. Has wings formed of skin membranes, but also tight, downy plumage and four pretty, ribbon-like tail feathers.

SIZE: Positively minute for a dinosaur at 32 inches (80cm) in length and just 13 ounces (380g) in weight

PROS: Small; short, dense feathers so it doesn't shed much around the house

CONS: Prone to screechiness; needs large aviary to glide back and forth within

Compsognathus

The smallest known dinosaur until the 1990s, when a variety of dainty, feathered relatives began to turn up in China. Also feathered and very lightly built, so great for small apartments.

SIZE: Turkey-sized but much daintier; up to 3 feet (1m) in length but just 7 pounds (3kg) in weight

PROS: Small size makes it an ideal lap-dinosaur; pack-living so highly social

CONS: Needs constant supply of small, live lizards to snack upon; bit of a finger nibbler

Without the dinosaurs disappearing, mammals would not have had the same opportunity.

Brusatte. "The asteroid was one of those dominoes that set in motion a chain of events that led to us. Without the dinosaurs disappearing, mammals would not have had the same opportunity."

He argues that mammals had already existed with dinosaurs for 160 million years or more when the asteroid struck. But they were mostly "marginal, shadowy little creatures" and—had the asteroid not caused a mass extinction—would likely remain that way today.

As Brusatte points out, "What's another 66 million years when it had already been like that for 160 million years already?"

STEGOSAURUS

WITH HUGE, RIGID PLATES ALONG ITS BACK AND SHARP SPINES ON ITS TAIL, THIS HERBIVORE COULD FEND OFF LETHAL ATTACKS.

THE ARRANGEMENT OF FOUR SPINES ON THE TAIL IS CALLED A "THAGOMIZER."

Stegosaurus is famed for its two rows of tall, thin plates lining its back that were embedded in the skin above its spine, rather than directly attached to the skeleton itself. Why they evolved is still a bit of a mystery. Most probably they were used for display, but also possibly for controlling body temperature. *Stegosaurus* used the four sharp spines on its tail tip (collectively called a "thagomizer") to protect itself from attacking predators like *Allosaurus* and *Ceratosaurus*.

THE BACK LEGS WERE LONGER THAN THE FRONT LEGS.

APPROXIMATE SIZE COMPARISON

FOUND IN USA

THE DIAMOND-SHAPED PLATES ALONG ITS BACK COULD HAVE BEEN USED FOR DISPLAY OR THERMAL REGULATION.

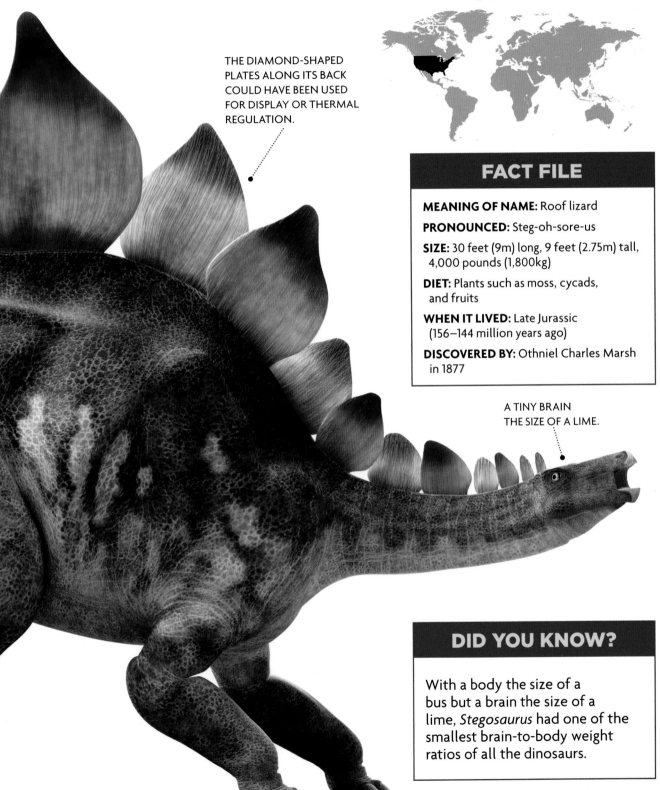

A TINY BRAIN THE SIZE OF A LIME.

FACT FILE

MEANING OF NAME: Roof lizard

PRONOUNCED: Steg-oh-sore-us

SIZE: 30 feet (9m) long, 9 feet (2.75m) tall, 4,000 pounds (1,800kg)

DIET: Plants such as moss, cycads, and fruits

WHEN IT LIVED: Late Jurassic (156–144 million years ago)

DISCOVERED BY: Othniel Charles Marsh in 1877

DID YOU KNOW?

With a body the size of a bus but a brain the size of a lime, *Stegosaurus* had one of the smallest brain-to-body weight ratios of all the dinosaurs.

Stegosaurus

HOW WE'LL BUILD THE REAL JURASSIC WORLD

With the *Jurassic Park* book and film series being so popular, have you been wondering if we really could bring extinct animals back from the dead?

Text by Brian Clegg, a science writer whose most recent book is *Big Data*
Illustrations by Andy Potts

How to Bring Back Extinct Creatures

Dinosaurs have captured imaginations for decades, but recreating them is a formidable challenge. *Jurassic Park* author Michael Crichton suggested getting dino DNA from blood-sucking insects that had been preserved in amber. The good news is that amber (fossilized tree sap) does sometimes contain well-preserved insects. The bad news is we can't get useful DNA this way. The problem is the half-life of DNA molecules.

DNA is a complex, fragile substance. Over time it breaks down, becoming less and less readable. A team from the University of Copenhagen and Murdoch University in Perth found that in 521 years, half of a sample of DNA would be broken into useless fragments, after another 521 years another half, and so on. This means that no part of a DNA sequence would be readable after 1.5 million years—far less than the 60 million-plus required for resurrecting a dinosaur. Furthermore, a team at Manchester University that tried the insect-in-amber technique found that DNA degraded faster than normal in these conditions.

But there is hope for recently extinct mammals like the thylacine (Tasmanian tiger), which died out in the early twentieth century, or even 5,000-year-old mammoths, found preserved in permafrost. Not only can researchers find intact DNA to use, but there are also closer living relatives to act as host mothers. In fact, Professor Michael Archer of the University of New South Wales believes bringing back the thylacine is a distinct possibility.

"I'm hopeful, given the increasing frequency of major technological breakthroughs in synthetic biology, that it will be within the next 20 years," he says.

Some believe we will never clone a mammoth, despite there being two projects underway attempting just this. Other experts such as Dr. Beth Shapiro, Associate Professor of Molecular Evolution at the University of California, Santa Cruz, are cautiously optimistic.

"It depends on what you are willing to call a mammoth," she explains. "If you are willing to accept an Asian elephant whose genome contains a very small amount of mammoth DNA— perhaps a few mammoth genes inserted in place of

Human persecution wiped out the thylacine.

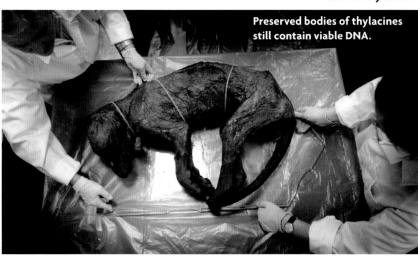

Preserved bodies of thylacines still contain viable DNA.

Dr. Beth Shapiro thinks that reverse engineering could help with de-extinction.

a kind of immune system, allowing bacteria to resist invasion by viruses. In the past couple of years, it's become evident that the CRISPR-Cas system can be used for the precision editing of genetic material . . . in the science-fictional world of dinosaur genome reconstruction, it would be an essential part of the toolkit."

It might seem that an approximation to a dinosaur would be a pretty worthless animal, but Gee disagrees. "Given that almost everything we know about dinosaurs comes from bones, and everything else is a matter of guesswork anyway, who's to notice the difference?" he asks.

Dino hybrids would allow researchers to explore the realities of dinosaur life, which currently we can only guess at from the fragmentary remains we have.

But not every expert is hopeful of success. Michael Benton, Professor of Vertebrate Paleontology at the University of Bristol, thinks that practicalities would overwhelm any attempt to manufacture a dinosaur.

"Reverse engineering DNA could be done now by snipping out bits and inserting bits, but who is to provide the pattern for DNA of any dinosaur? I can see no way we can provide even a faint guess at their genome," he says. "Why bother? And, if we could, surely we have more important purposes to which to put the technology—like engineering out disease or engineering in food productivity."

Predictably, Shapiro is more hopeful. "We now know the complete genome sequences of more than 50 species of birds, as well as alligators and crocodiles," she says. "Using these data, we can reconstruct, using a computer and models of how genomes change over time, what the most likely sequence of the common ancestor of birds was. We might then go into the genome sequence of a living bird and change it so that it looks like this common ancestor. For now, this is a thought experiment, of course."

the elephant version of genes, so that an elephant is better able to survive in a cold place—then this could happen quite quickly. For mammoth de-extinction, the biggest challenge is probably not sequencing and assembling DNA or editing an elephant genome so that it looks more mammoth-like, but the later stages—implanting a developing embryo in a surrogate mom, having that pregnancy develop to term, rearing a newborn calf. These are challenges that not only do we not know how to solve, but that, ethically, remain questionable."

It would be remarkable if these extinct mammals were brought to life, but it isn't *Jurassic Park*. Dinosaurs have a unique fascination and are the most attractive possibility for creation. And although it is not currently possible, what is proposed is "dinosaur light." This would be a hybrid of an existing animal and a dinosaur.

Starting with the DNA of an animal descended from dinosaurs—a big bird, for instance—scientists would try to produce the characteristics we know, or suspect, dinosaurs had by genetic engineering. The result might be something that looked and acted like a *Tyrannosaurus rex*, but that would not truly be one.

"CRISPR, Clustered Regularly Interspersed Short Palindromic Repeats, are short gene-like sequences. They are often associated with a particular enzyme, Cas," explains paleontologist Dr. Henry Gee. "The CRISPR-Cas system—found naturally in bacteria—is

While such a technique is not possible today, the rate of advances in gene technology means it may be conceivable in 50 years. And, considering our love affair with dinosaurs, how could we resist?

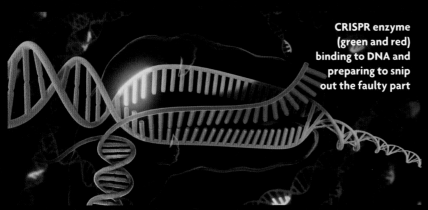

CRISPR enzyme (green and red) binding to DNA and preparing to snip out the faulty part

The last mammoth population lived on Wrangel Island, 87 miles (140km) off the coast of northeast Siberia, and died out around 4,000 years ago.

How to Rear Dinosaurs to Maturity

Even with dinosaur DNA, the route to a fully grown animal is complex. "To work properly, DNA has to be packaged," explains paleontologist Dr. Henry Gee. "Many parts of DNA are coiled around protein complexes called histones. The degree to which DNA is wrapped around histones has a bearing on which genes are turned on during development and when."

Gee adds that much of DNA is modified chemically, as part of a pattern called the epigenome. This is also vital in development. "The most important thing, however, is the early maternal environment. The earliest stages in the development of an embryo depend on chemical factors left in the egg by the mother. Even having the right factors in the right places

Not all dinosaur eggs were as big as these.

within the egg is important," explains Gee. "As we don't have fresh dinosaur eggs to work with, we'd have to use crocodile or bird eggs. Scientists know an awful lot about chicken eggs, so perhaps they'd start with those."

Luckily, not all dinosaurs were on the scale of *Diplodocus*—there were plenty of chicken-sized dinosaurs that we could experiment with before jumping straight to the big boys. When it comes to rearing, we would need to be aware of species requirements—just as with birds.

"We know that some dinosaurs behaved very like birds with respect to nesting and incubation," says Gee. "We also know that reproductively active female dinosaurs underwent secondary remodeling of their bones, associated with providing calcium for the eggshells and embryos. So, in some cases at least, birds and dinosaurs behaved very similarly. But dinosaurs were very diverse, and it is possible that they had a range of reproductive habits, from full-on parental care, to laying eggs in a nest or mound and forgetting all about them."

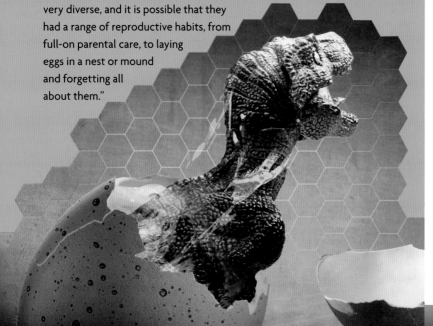

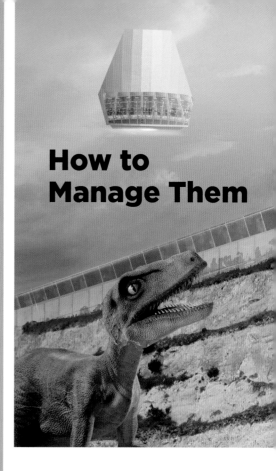

How to Manage Them

The owners of a dinosaur reserve would need to keep their animals safe and happy, while giving visitors a chance to see them as close-up as possible. The European Association of Zoos and Aquaria (EAZA) produces a detailed file on the management of each major species called an EEP (European Endangered Species Programme), which would need to include dinosaurs.

The difficulties of handling large dinosaurs are likely to be surprisingly similar to those faced when looking after large mammals—a fully grown male African elephant can weigh up to 7.7 tons (7 tonnes), a similar weight to a *T. rex*. Although a large, grazing sauropod like a *Diplodocus* could weigh up to three times as much, they would be far slower. They would, therefore, provide less of an issue for any barrier than a high-speed predator. In practice, it's likely that the dinosaurs could be kept in place by using concrete and rock barriers.

Bob Lawrence, Head of Wildlife Development at West Midland Safari Park, points out that one vital aspect of keeping animals secure is understanding the social grouping of the particular species. For example, some tolerate a male hierarchy, but others only allow one mature male in a group. The latter

scenario would result in battles where the loser would attempt to flee and could try to charge out of the enclosure, putting the containment under stress. With our limited understanding of dinosaur social groupings, there would be an initial need for an environment where security was key to avoid escapes.

Elephants are often confined using electric fences, but Lawrence points out that not only are these potentially inhumane, but more intelligent species can find ways to disrupt them. Elephants have been known to short them out using tree branches, and there is always the possibility of technical failure. Steel barriers or high walls would need to be capable of withstanding the impact of charging dinosaurs. When housing elephants, about 8 feet (2.5m) is the recommended minimum height for a barrier, but in the case of taller dinosaurs, this would have to be increased appropriately.

For smaller predators like *Velociraptor*, Lawrence recommends the kind of fencing used for wolves, which typically involves a 45-degree inward overhang. This is essential when the animals can be good jumpers.

Lawrence recommends siting a dinosaur park in an old quarry,

According to Bob Lawrence, we must understand social groupings to keep animals safe and secure.

For continuity, *Jurassic World*'s producers stuck with scaly dinosaurs like those above, but the fossil record suggests *Velociraptor* and many other dinosaurs had feathers.

such as the disused chalk pits in Kent, England. These can have sides over 98 feet (30m) deep, keeping the animals safe from escape. It would also be much more secure than using an island to confine species when we don't know how well they'd cope with water. "We were caught out once when we didn't realize that wallabies could swim. We used an island to confine them and within 24 hours they all swam off," Lawrence explains.

For smaller dinosaurs, existing bird enclosures would likely prove fine. "One might have greater success with some of the smaller, feathered dinosaurs, no bigger than crows or pigeons, which could be kept in an aviary," says Gee.

For a thylacine, the issues would be similar to those in breeding any large animal. "The same issues would need to be addressed, including optimizing genetic diversity and acclimatization to the attributes of potential release habitats," says Archer. "For some animals and plants, a parallel conservation strategy might involve enabling suitable species to become human companions.

FIVE FREEDOMS

ZOOKEEPERS REFER TO THE FIVE FREEDOMS OF ANIMALS, WHICH WOULD INEVITABLY BE EXTENDED TO DINOSAURS. THESE ARE:

1. Freedom from hunger and thirst
Adequate, well-balanced, and timed nutrition must be provided.

2. Freedom from discomfort
A suitable environment with shelter and appropriate materials allows animals to live as closely as possible to a natural environment.

3. Freedom from pain, injury and disease
Animals should not be put at risk by the enclosure and should have good access to veterinary medicine.

4. Freedom from fear and distress
These can be avoided by providing correct grouping and sex ratios, and including an appropriate mix of species. There should be a lack of unnecessary confinement and places to escape from view.

5. Freedom to behave normally
In old-fashioned zoo environments, animals would pace unnaturally. Instead, they should have somewhere to express their natural behavior as closely as possible.

If this had been legal when thylacines were being kept as pets in Tasmania, it's depressingly clear that the thylacine would not be extinct today. There are lessons to be learned from this tragedy, based on the erroneous presumption that wildlife is always safest in the wild."

There is always going to be compromise, but good zoos and wildlife parks will have the animals' welfare at their heart. The trouble with dinosaurs is that so much would initially be a matter of guesswork.

Take *T. rex*. For years, this dinosaur with immensely powerful jaws was considered a straightforward predator. We now know it also scavenged and lived off the kills of others, like a hyena. Yet some paleontologists believe it was almost entirely a scavenger. There is evidence to support both theories, which is typical of the uncertainty we face.

Equally, there is some evidence that *T. rex* indulged in cannibalism. After years of hard work, it would hardly be great news if one specimen ate the rest. Similarly, although it has been suggested that dinosaurs were less susceptible to disease than mammals, this is based on inference from the fossil record, which is patchy in the extreme.

Computer modeling suggests that an adult *T. rex* could bite with a force of over 5.5 tons (5 tonnes).

With very large animals, there is also the problem of getting enough food into the enclosure at a time. A *T. rex* would probably need 40,000 calories a day, equivalent to eating a large goat. There's no reason why it couldn't cope with modern meat, though if it proved to be primarily a scavenger, it would be more likely to be fed with, say, a cow carcass on a less frequent basis. Any sensible *T. rex* facility would have a failsafe mechanism for delivering food without having to risk physically entering the enclosure.

A large herbivore like *Diplodocus* probably had a diet of ferns and soft leaves—there would be considerably more concern about finding appropriate diets (think, for example, how fussy a panda is in requiring bamboo shoots). But whatever the exact plant life involved, an animal with this bulk would need large quantities of vegetation—perhaps 0.55 ton (0.5 tonne) per day. In this case, the supply might be challenging, but at least the enclosure can be entered with less risk.

Currently, we know so little for sure. This is why, even if they weren't perfect, the idea of creating dinosaur hybrids could help paleontologists get a better picture of Jurassic and Cretaceous life.

WHO WOULD RUN THE PARK?

WHILE NONE OF THESE INDIVIDUALS IS INVOLVED IN CREATING A DINOSAUR ATTRACTION, THEY'RE EXACTLY THE KIND OF PEOPLE SUCH A VENTURE WOULD NEED.

DR. BETH SHAPIRO

The Ancient DNA Expert

Recreating dinosaurs would mean finding out as much as we could about their DNA and reverse engineering what we couldn't find. An expert in ancient DNA is an essential cast member, and Shapiro already has a project working on a form of reverse engineering.

PROFESSOR MICHAEL ARCHER

The De-Extinction Expert

Archer and a small number of individuals are looking at the practicalities of producing a living specimen of an extinct creature. The work currently focuses on recently extinct mammals, but for the park that would have to be extended much further.

PROFESSOR MICHAEL BENTON

The Paleontologist

We can't get anywhere without an expert in dinosaurs. These scientists can help us discover remnants and will increase our understanding as much as possible. They can teach us about the life cycles of the animals to give us the best chance of successfully rearing them.

CLIVE PALMER

The Backer

This eccentric Australian mining billionaire is exactly the kind of backer that would be essential to get an ambitious project like this off the ground, as it would require a huge amount of funding. According to the Australian press, Mr. Palmer has already expressed an interest in cloning dinosaurs.

SIR RICHARD BRANSON

The Showman

There is no doubt that the Virgin owner is an ultimate showman, and he already owns a private game reserve, Ulusaba in South Africa, adjoining the Kruger National Park. Sir Richard's ebullient enthusiasm and media access make him an ideal candidate for launching a dinosaur park.

How We'll Build the Real Jurassic World

Where to Put the Park and How to Engineer a Habitat

We tend to lump together dinosaurs as a single group of animals—but they lived over a huge time period from the Jurassic (200–145 million years ago) when massive herbivores like *Diplodocus* were common, through to the late Cretaceous (101–66 million years ago), when the likes of *Velociraptor* and *T. rex* thrived. Not surprisingly, the habitats varied. But generally the need would be for a warm, humid environment with plenty of coniferous trees and fern plantations.

However, it isn't always essential to match a habitat to an animal. With suitable winter protection, African animals can survive comfortably in British safari parks. And it may be that dinosaurs would be equally adaptable, although this is something that would require experiments with living animals to determine. With this in mind, the first park would require highly controlled and large-scale environments. As such, it wouldn't really matter where in the world the park was situated. The driving factor would more likely be the source of funding.

The key to the adaptability of the animals would be whether they resembled warm-blooded birds or cold-blooded reptiles. A fully warm-blooded organism can cope with much wider ranges of climate, whereas cold-blooded animals require a more controlled temperature range to thrive. Although we have moved away from the idea that dinosaurs were cold-blooded, we still don't know for sure whether something like a *T. rex* had a full-scale warm-blooded metabolism or something in between the two, leaving it more susceptible to the cold. The only way we can find out for sure is by experiment.

Modern birds are descended from a group of dinos called theropods.

We could safely explore a dinosaur attraction in transparent pods, like the ones featured in *Jurassic World*.

Visitor Experience

Dinosaurs would be so valuable that the visitor experience would come second to security. Good walls, designed to look like natural structures, with viewing points and ports would give the best combination of safety and access. In a future Eden Project-style environment, there could be virtual robotic tours of the enclosures and the ability to fly over the top in a totally transparent vehicle.

We know already from dinosaur exhibitions that there will be plenty of spinoffs.

It's unlikely that the park's restaurant would serve actual mammoth or dinosaur burgers, but it would be possible to use the same technology that produced a $262,000 (£200,000) lab-grown burger to grow mammoth and dinosaur meat—there is talk of the price dropping to under $13 (£10) in the next few years. To accompany their meal, visitors might like a glass of the Fossil Fuels Brewing Company's beer, claimed to be made using a yeast strain dating back 45 million years.

No doubt dinosaur toys making realistic sounds would be popular—but as yet, we have little idea of the noises that dinosaurs made. There has been speculation that strange bony head crests on some duck-billed dinosaurs were used to create resonant cries, but most dinosaur noises featured in movies are not particularly accurate.

Paleontologist Phil Senter has suggested that dinosaurs may not have had cries at all. This is because their two living descendants, the birds and crocodylians, have totally different sound-making mechanisms from each other, suggesting their common ancestor may have had neither. Anyway, after the noise of the *Velociraptor* claws on the floor in *Jurassic Park* gave everyone nightmares, you may be thinking twice about a dino attraction.

Microbiologist Raul Cano isolated ancient yeast to make Fossil Fuels beer.